INTEGRITY - INTEGRITY:
In Times Like These?

By

Frank C. Wilson

Editor

Frank C. Wilson, Jr.

OTHER BOOKS
BY FRANK C. WILSON

Industrial Cost Controls, Prentice-Hall, Inc., Englewood Cliffs, NJ 07632, Second Printing, 1973

Short-Term Financial Management, Dow Jones-Irwin, Inc. Homewood, IL 60430, Second Printing, 1981

Production Planning and Control Handbook, Prentice-Hall, Inc., Englewood Cliffs, NJ 07632, First Printing, 1980

Managing Costs and Improving Cash Flow, Dow Jones-Irwin, Homewood, IL 60430, Third Printing, 2000

DEDICATION

This book is dedicated to my wife
of 55 years, Anne, who made
my life Heaven on Earth.

Anne Richardson Jones Wilson
March 17th, 1927 - Clio, SC
September 23rd, 2006 - Gainesville, GA.

Visit www.booksurge.com to order additional copies.

ACKNOWLEDGEMENTS

In preparing this manuscript, the participation and help of my family, Anne, Lynn and Chip, has been a treasure of good to me. My son, Chip Wilson, made significant improvements as Editor.

If this book helps one person do a better job, work in peace, find Christ - it will be a success.

My secretary, Mrs. Malcolm Lathem, never lost patience with my many drafts, and her constant help enabled the completion of this book.

Dan Johnson worked patiently with me installing a new computer system, scanning typed material into Windows and assisting in many other ways. Without Dan, this book would never have been completed. Mrs. Carol Rascoe's suggestions and encouragement helped me push on to complete this writing. Ruth Anne and Paul Drechsel's corrections and improvements were invaluable,

Special acknowledgment is given to Dr. James T. Fischer, M. D. and Lowell S. Hawley whose

book, <u>A Few Buttons Missing</u>, published by
J. P. Lippincott Co., New York, 1951, 12th Printing was very helpful. Some sentences and para-
graphs are used as a result of the excellence of
these authors' writing.

ABOUT THE AUTHOR

Frank C. Wilson is a Certified Management Consultant, Registered Professional Engineer, Certified Cost Engineer and Registered Land Surveyor with over fifty years experience in business, working with executives and managers at all levels at home and abroad.

Wilson is a graduate of Auburn University with a BS of Industrial Management and the Graduate School of the Georgia Institute of Technology with a MS of Industrial Engineering with other study at New York University. He has been selected for a number of professional, industry, and honorary achievements and organization

He has been invited to speak and teach throughout much of the western world. He is the author of four books - Industrial Cost

Controls, Prentice-Hall, Inc., Short Term Financial Management, Dow Jones-Irwin, Inc., Production Planning and Control Handbook, Prentice Hall, Inc. and Managing Costs And Improving Cash Flow, Dow Jones-Irwin, Inc.

Wilson has written hundreds of articles published throughout North America and internationally. He was a periodic guest editorial writer for THE TIMES, Gainesville, Georgia. He had short term teaching assignments at Georgia Tech and Piedmont College.

He has conducted over 150 seminars for businesses, universities and trade organizations in the US, Canada, Scandinavia and Europe. These include the Georgia Institute of Technology, Clemson University, the University of Alabama for NASA, the American Management Association, and others.

PREFACE

Can a Christian succeed in business?

Christian business people - in the office, on the factory floor or in the field – have some of the hardest jobs on earth. They are torn by the conflicting demands placed on them by employees for higher earnings, by stockholders for profits, by customers for service, by a community for activities, and by their family for a whole life. The opportunity to cheat on production and deliver an inferior product in order to make a profit by questionable means is ever present.

Trained to use scientific methods, systematic and professional management systems, computers, engineering, and statistical economic models, the manager is in conflict with the demands on themselves, the ethics of business, and Christian beliefs.

The ever accelerating pace of information – e-mails, text messages, cell phones and twitters - erode a manager's time with employees and on the factory floor. Time is spent in the office answering e-mails rather than being out where the people are working. E-mails and similar communications techniques have replaced the need for face-to-face contacts and more personal telephone calls. Issues have replaced problems. Even on weekends, holidays and anywhere in the world, the manager is on duty with cell phones, Palm Pilots and other devices.

How does an executive respond when one person on his staff is using company politics to obtain a better position? Why do some executives accept salaries, benefits, and retirement packages worth millions or hundreds of millions of dollars when the worker on the factory floor is often on a tight budget fighting inflation?

Why do businesses provide multi-million dollar aircraft to fly a few people (often family members) into an airport and take up the same airspace as a Boeing 747 with hundreds of passengers? Is it selfishness or effectiveness? One thing I have learned is that everyone in business is expendable, including top managers and executives. Why do some fail in business for ''being too good, or to soft-hearted?''

In the lions den of business can a Christian succeed?

The news media is filled with the terrors and anxieties of wars around the world. Sometimes, "wars" in business between people striving to gain advantage, between divisions in a firm, and between competitors, can be brutal and just as devastating as shooting wars. Lives can waste away, health can be ruined, mental anguish can destroy a nervous system, and yet business continues as usual. A whole manager is required in the broken world of business - broken ethics, broken integrity, and broken trust.

These questions, and many others, that have arisen in over fifty years in business, teaching and writing, as an employee and as an individual consultant in North America and many other countries have prompted this book. I have sought ways out of these dilemmas, and many others, that managers have had in business.

Once, I believed education, knowledge, better management, operations research, the scientific method, economics, finance, marketing, sales, and other things were the answers. Yet, as I moved into the larger realm, these skills - although helpful - were found to be incomplete and inadequate.

I explored all the alternatives. Then events occurred in my life which changed my perspective – from self to Christ, from me to others. I was no longer alone!

Publications abound concerning the pressures facing almost everyone in business - the effect on the person, the effect on the body's mechanics, and stress. Excessive stress affects almost every aspect of our existence. Literature is plentiful (some I have written) on how to manage, how to be a professional systematic manager and how to be an effective executive. Yet, to try to change business practices by improving the effectiveness of managers without changing business morality is insane.

This book is for the manager - as a person, an individual, and a human - rather than a job title, or a collective part of a committee or corporation.

Managers are besieged by terms - marketing concept, job enrichment, management information centers, and programs like Six Sigma - which seem to be the answers to problems. A manager sometimes looks to these and other techniques, as solutions to the difficulties surrounding him or her and to help him or her set priorities. Caught in the whirlpool of crisis with the lonely feeling of standing in quicksand, are there any absolutes left as a basis for management in this age?

This book is not an answer; it is not a guideline or a check list. It does explore and face up to some of the situations that are unmentionable in the executive peer group. This book is not a sophisticated, theoretical examination. It is a practical, common sense, down to earth, approach to management today. It provides a basis to help absorb the shock of the ever accelerating pace of business.

Short, precise, and straight to the point, the thoughts in these pages are designed to use the manger's time very effectively. The examples and illustrations are from the real world. Each is true! They are so well camouflaged that the individuals themselves will not recognize the situations. The examples are typical of those that managers encounter - today.

This book is another step in the fight to replace ulcers with confidence, failure with hope, and turmoil with security. It is a way out of the labyrinth of frustration - a way to find the eye of the needle to a meaningful victorious life in the world of business.

Why is a book oriented toward a Christian approach to business needed? Almost all of us will spend the rest of our lives associated with a business system in some way - as a customer, an employee or an employer. Business and capitalism are the foundation of the free enterprise system.

These case studies are geared to the executive at the top, to the middle manager, to the new person starting the climb up the business ladder, and to those who look at managers from the outside. This book is for all those in management, and for all those contemplating a business career.

You and I have a responsibility to be a Christian in business. We have the opportunity to witness and live for Christ. As the Rev. Ben, Haden has said, "The business world is the greatest mission field on earth, the greatest platform for witnessing for Christ. In our job, we are subbing for Christ."

Some think that moralism – doing good, helping others, etc. - defines a Christian. Moralism is good, but inadequate. A true Christian accepts Christ in his heart and has joy in His eternal salvation.

In a world torn by war, by insecurity, by changing values and by an economy in a recession or depression, is it possible to be a Christian in business and be a success?

YES!

I believe that for two thousand years, the Christian world has been holding in its hands the complete answer to our restless and fruitless yearnings. Here, with Jesus Christ, is the blueprint for success in human life – at home and in business.

Author's Note:

Some of the case studies are the personal experiences of the author.

Though all case studies are true, the author does not accept any responsibility or liability should anyone or firm think a case study applies to them or their business.

TABLE OF CONTENTS

1 INTEGRITY – INTEGRITY: IN TIMES LIKE THESE?

"Buckle on the belt of truth, Put on the coat of integrity."

Ephesians 6:14

CHAPTER ONE

INTEGRITY - INTEGRITY: IN TIMES LIKE THESE?

"Buckle on the belt of truth. Put on the coat of integrity."

Ephesians 6:14

"Governor Accused in Scheme to Sell Obama's Seat" (Ref.1, 2 and 3) were the headlines. One governor (Republican) is serving a sentence and the current governor (Democrat) is indicted on a wide range of charges. The longest serving US Senator, at the age of 84, indicted for not reporting gifts.

A Committee Chairman in the House fails to report rental income. A Secretary of the Treasury designate neglects to pay his self-employment tax plus forgot to check the immigration status of a person working in his household who was an illegal alien. Are these situations a part of a culture of political corruption or brazen stupidity?

A hugely successful and respected Wall Street legend whose firm employed hundreds of traders arrested and accused of conducting a multi-billion-dollar criminal securities fraud – a Ponzi scheme – perhaps the largest in Wall Streets history, approaching $60-billion (Ref.4 & 5). The S.E.C.'s assistant director of the regional office called it, "a stunning fraud that appears to be of epic proportions." At the age of 70 and decades of success, what would drive a person to these illegal actions?

Executives run a firm into disaster and walk away with millions of dollars in severance payments. A financial analyst develops risky investments like credit default swaps and derivatives, takes home big bonuses and lets the taxpayers pay the bill.

Government enterprises guarantee loans for homes with no verification of income or assets valuation leaving honest citizens who pay their bills and taxes facing lenders with huge uncollectible liabilities. Major companies make mistakes over decades, pay excessive salaries and benefits to their executives and then expect the government (TAXPAYERS) to bail them out.

Some of Wall Street's savviest investors were swindled out of hundreds of millions of dollars by a trusted lawyer with offices in six cities with and over two hundred attorneys on his staff (Ref. 6). The high profile lawyer sold fake promissory notes to his clients. The accused was a Yale graduate and Harvard educated lawyer. He owned a Manhattan triplex, a waterfront home in the Hamptons and a place on Ocean Avenue in Santa Monica, CA. He had a Mercedes 500 in New York and an Aston Martin in California. His 121 foot Hessen motor yacht with a Jacuzzi and crew of ten was docked in either Manhattan or St. Martens. All of his employees became suddenly unemployed with no liability insurance to protect them from their client legal actions. How much is enough?

A major international corporation fined $1.6-billion for bribery. Managers had an annual fund of $40-50-million to bribe officials to obtain contracts from Russia, China, Vietnam and other countries. The executive of another well known firm admits using bribery to get contracts plus skimming off millions for himself (Ref. 7).

❦❦

How can so many of our best and brightest be so brazenly stupid and/or greedy and/or slaves to sin?

❦❦

A professor who exposes fraud in grades of football players is demoted and fired (Ref. 8). She and other faculty members complained to officials at the university that nine football players had been given passing grades in a remedial English course which they had failed. After a jury found that the professor was fired illegally, she was reinstated and awarded a $1.08-million dollar settlement. The President of the University resigned, but the winning football coach continued to win games for many years until retirement.

Speaker of the House of Commons in United Kingdom, the first in 300 years, is forced out of office – a historic departure (Ref. 9). The last resignation was Sir John Trevor in 1696. Members of the House of Commons were allowed to charge personal and other dubious expenses on their Commons expense accounts. One member charged a 42-inch plasma TV, leather bed and hundreds of UK pounds of furniture. Another member spent thousands of pounds of public funds on mortgage interest payments, redecoration and furnishings for a flat where his daughter now lives. And, another member charged 62,000 pounds (approximately $100,000, May 2009) in expenses for his London flat for four years, which had a mortgage of 26,000 pounds.

The list is endless of members of the House of Commons involved in this scandal at the expense of the public taxpayers. Other members of Parliament are in a sense of panic waiting to see who else will be involved in these thefts of public money. Where were their ethics? What were those in charge doing to protect the public? What happened to the commandment, "Thou shall not steal?"

A manager leaves his wife for another employee; both leave broken homes and children. Teenagers and adults become alcoholics and drug addicts. Too much stuff and too much money, most on credit, have made us a spoiled generation.

Financial systems go to pieces; the Federal Reserve and Treasury Department throw money in every direction. The only way to create trillions of dollars is to assume debt or to print dollars. The value of the dollar will eventually slide or even collapse. Then, the government will simply move the decimal point on the dollar one or two digits to the left (example: France after WWII) and other countries. In our case, a $10.00 bill may simply become $1.00.

Integrity – Integrity: In Times Like These? Does anyone know right from wrong?

If one traces the history of the Roman Empire, we will find that at the peak of its power, the currency was 100 percent gold. As the gold content was lowered, eventually to zero, the empire collapsed (Exhibit in Bath, England). Since we are no longer on the gold standard, can a similar thing happen to the powerful United States of America? YES!

What has happened to integrity in government, in business and in us? Surely, Sodom and Gomorrah could not have been much worse. But, there is hope. God has promised to protect His remnant. And, there is a remnant made up of Christians.

Integrity is defined by a Random House Dictionary as "soundness of and adherence to moral principle and character; uprightness; honesty." But, where are we to get these moral principles? They will not be found on the internet, TV, iPod, video games or most current publications. Limit sports viewing and only watch or go to movies with moral teachings.

There are very, very few acceptable movies. One of the exceptions is "Fireproof" (Ref. 10). Leave alcohol and drugs. Stay off the video games! Violence, sex and filthy language are not the foundation of integrity.

The Bible and the teachings of Christ are the source of eternal moral principles, honesty and uprightness – integrity. We can start with the Ten Commandments or the Sermon on the Mount. We can read the Bible through or listen on CD's, attend a Bible believing church with a Pastor that believes all the Bible is the word of God and takes seriously what he has declared about his son.

Some words from God's Word, the Bible – (Job 2:3), "Job is a blameless and upright man, one who fears God and shuns evil. He holds fast to his integrity." (Proverbs 11:3), "The integrity of the upright will guide them. But, the perversity of the unfaithful will destroy them." (Titus 2:7), "In all things, show yourself to be a pattern of good works; in doctrine showing integrity, reverence, incorruptibility, sound speech that cannot be condemned, that one who is an opponent has nothing evil to say of you." And, others . . .

ⓒⓢ

The Bible is either true or false.

ⓒⓢ

There is a heaven and hell or there is not. The probability is either 1.00 or 0.00. When we breathe our last breath, we will go to one or the other for eternity. There is no in-between. None of us know when our lives will end. Today is the day, this is the minute, to rethink where we are and where we will be going at life's end!

There are many reasons for optimism. Sadly, our news media thrives on bad news. We can find a local church with the right theology. It is not the music, though much is to be learned from hymns like Amazing Grace and others, it is the message, the theology. You will be able to find a local church which is one of God's remnants.

Visit a local college and on many campuses, particularly Bible Colleges, and you will be impressed by the student body and their talents. Some of these outstanding young people are God's Christian remnant. They will replace some of our spoiled generation.

I believe that for 2,000 years, the Christian world has been holding in its hands the complete answer to our restless and fruitless yearnings. Here, with Christ, rests the blueprint for a successful and satisfying human life. Here, too, is the only pathway to eternity in Heaven with Christ.

Ref. 1: Davey, Monica, "Governor Accused in Scheme to Sell Obama's Seat," NEW YORK TIMES, December 10th, 2008, Page A1.

Ref. 2: Weltzman, Hai, "Illinois governor charged over Obama seat sale," FINANCIAL TIMES, December 10th, 2008, Page 1.

Ref. 3: Belkin, Douglas, "Governor Jailed in Alleged Graft Spree," WALL STREET JOURNAL, December 10th, 208, Page A1.

Ref. 4: Henriques, Diana, "Top Trader Is Accused of Defrauding Clients," NEW YORK TIMES, December 12, 2008, Page B1.

Ref.5: Efratit, A., "Top Trader Accused of Fraud," WALL STREET JOURNAL, Page A1.

Ref. 6: Cowan, Allison, "A Lawyer Seen as Bold Enough To Cheat the Best of Investors," NEW YORK TIMES, December 14, 2008, Page A1.

Ref. 7: Schubert, Siri, "Siemens: Where Bribery Was Just a Line Item," NEW YORK TIMES, December 21, 2008, Sunday Business, Page 1.

Ref. 8: "Jan Kemp, 59, Exposed Fraud in Grades of Players," NEW YORK TIMES, December 11, 2008, Page B11.

Ref. 9: Porter, Andrew, "MPs' expenses: Michael Martin becomes first Commons Speaker to quit in 300 years," TELEGRAPH.co.uk, London, May 20, 2009

Ref. 10: "Fireproof", Sherwood Baptist Church, Albany, GA, 2008.

2 NEIGHBORHOOD OF STRANGERS

"Do not forget to entertain strangers, for by so doing some have unwittingly entertained angels."

Hebrews 13:2

CHAPTER TWO

NEIGHBORHOOD OF STRANGERS

"Do not forget to entertain strangers,
for by so doing some have unwittingly
entertained angel."

Hebrews 13:2

Hillside Drive curves its way past neat lots
with a variety of home styles and almost identical mailboxes. An occasional tree is beginning
to grow in the Crestview Terrace Subdivision as
the bulldozers cleared the site some years ago
for the construction of middle class homes.

The people you meet may be from Jackson,
Mississippi, San Diego, California and Albany,
New York. Yet, none are at ease in the city in
which the Crestview Subdivision is located.

Only ten years ago cattle grazed on the
slopes and the sounds of birds could be heard
in the quiet atmosphere. But, the pastures disappeared beneath streets, driveways and patios.
Three hundred to five hundred thousand dollar

multistory homes replaced the weathered barns and the grassy landscapes.

Most homes were so close together that there were small grass yards and minimum landscaping. Families were too busy to enjoy yard work and gardening. With husbands and wives working to maintain a high standard of living and providing children with every opportunity - soccer games, school, and other scheduled activities compressed their day into a living for the moment life. There was no time to smell the roses.

They are transients - the people who live in these houses. They are part of the white column nomads. Some families move each year or two. For those who make neighborhoods like Hillside Drive, the present location is home for a little while as they await the next promotion or military transfer.

Most of the residents of the Crestview Subdivision have lived there less than two or three years. Many of them will be gone two years from now. Where is the moving van parked today?

When they leave, it will be very much as they came with few ties to the city or to the people who were their neighbors. Of thirty-three families, most of them had moved from one city to another since their marriage. Twenty-two of these families had moved from one city to another at least three times. Ten had moved five times or more. The thirty-three families represent fifteen states and one foreign country. No family had lived in Crestview Terrace more than three and one-half years.

The families of James Long and Joseph Parham moved to Crestview Terrace from Cleveland, Ohio last summer. Now, eight months later, they still do not know that each other exist - even though they live only six houses apart. They probably will never get to know each other well. James Long and his family are preparing for another move.

It is not the moving that bothers people in Crestview Terrace so much. It is the feeling of being a stranger in their own neighborhood, of having no roots, of constant uncertainty - never knowing when their boss will tell them that they must move again.

Many of the wives are lonely and feel isolated though a substantial proportion of them join churches, and are active in social or civic clubs. One wife stated, "It is not easy to get involved in a place where everybody is a stranger, even at church."

Moving is really hardest on the children. They do make new friends quickly; yet, they lose the loyalty, the sense of belonging, of being a lasting part of their school, a team or other peer group. Both parents and children tend to get less involved, accept less responsibility, and fail to contribute to the betterment of their neighborhood, and their community.

It is estimated that one in five of America's families move each year. And the statistic is moving to one in four. Their companies grow larger, as conglomerates extend across the nation; as multi-national corporations span the globe, the stability, the security - the very foundation of the American family weakens.

For this reason, some may say there is no need for a husband to accept every promotion. However, in the corporate black book, he will be marked down as one who refused an opportunity. For future promotions, he may simply be overlooked entirely.

Many wives of these white collar corporate nomads go to work for one reason alone–to break the isolation or "to have someone over six years old to talk to." Without foundation, without roots and with their mother at work, the opportunity for children to become juvenile delinquents exists at every turn. Alcohol is available in most homes and drugs can be obtained easily. Children come home from school to an empty home; they watch trash on television, play violent video games and explore the sometimes evil internet. Mother and father are not there to welcome them and guide them to proper activities like homework, sports and music.

Children are often the big losers in these lifestyles. The mother often returns to work in a few weeks after the baby is born. The child is dropped off at daycare on the way to work and picked up en-route home. The mother and father get home exhausted; then, they must prepare dinner and handle the family needs. If that is not enough, the father may be away on a business trip leaving everything to his wife.

There does not seem to be any corporate loyalty in these times. The wife often feels the need to have a job simply for security if the husband becomes unemployed. Who knows the results of the next year's job review?

There is always the question:

©©

How much wealth and status is enough?

©©

When do we put God, our family and our church ahead of this escalator living?

Sometimes it seems that corporations, and many business enterprises both large and small, are dedicated only to the profit motive - to maximize financial results. We in business have responsibilities to our employees to help them build a whole life, to our communities for good government, and to build a better society. Our business will operate more effectively under a stable environment in the office and in the home. Retaining capable people is the lubrication which permits a business to operate smoothly.

❧

Constant changes are the sands which grind into inefficiency.

❧

True - transfer and relocation of employees is essential from time to time. However, many of our transfers are unnecessary. How many moves could be avoided with prior planning? How many managers could be promoted in their present Division, their existing factory, or in their current geographical territory?

Helen and Jim Jones moved to Hillside Drive. During their first Christmas, they both were concerned that this was their daughter's sixth Christmas. And, she had always been in a different location for each of those six years. Jim's boss had already told him they wanted him to move again the next year, to get another promotion and higher salary.

Helen and Jim thought and prayed. They wanted their children to have a stable life. So,

Jim gave up the next promotion, the next move and resigned to start his own small business. The first years were tough, but they survived and eventually prospered. Both children went through the same school system and graduated from their high school with many good friends.

The beginning of the whole manager in a broken business world is security for his family, his job, and his business. Here, the Church of Christ and all Christians have a superior opportunity to witness for Christ, to minister to the loneliness of the corporate nomads, and to help them while they are in our midst.

3 SHE'S GOT LEUKEMIA

"We want you not to remain in ignorance, brothers, about those who sleep in death; you should not grieve like the rest of men, who have no hope. We believe that Christ died and rose again; and so it will be for those who died as Christians; God will bring them to life with Jesus."

1st Thessalonians 4:13-14

CHAPTER THREE

SHE'S GOT LEUKEMIA

"We want you not to remain in ignorance,
brothers, about those who sleep in death;
you should not grieve like the rest of
men, who have no hope. We believe that
Christ died and rose again; and so it will
be for those who died as Christians; God
will bring them to life with Jesus."

1st Thessalonians 4:13-14

Bill Nelson, President of a management consulting firm, direct-dialed a long-term client to
follow up on a routine problem. The secretary
recognized his voice and quickly put the call
through to Victor Zeller, President of Electron-
ics Corporation.

Victor Zeller and his family had reached
the top, socially and professionally. They had a
swimming pool in the back yard, a condominium in Florida and access to the corporate jet.
At forty-seven, Victor was secure financially, and
his plan called for early retirement at fifty five.

Two daughters, Jan and Sharon, were wonderful children. A son, Victor, Jr. was a successful college student,

The conversation about the problem for discussion went smoothly. Bill sensed a bit of distraction from Victor. In closing, he routinely asked, "How is the family? Is Sharon's basketball team still winning?" (She played first string for the high school team.)

The phony atmosphere broke as Victor explained, "She's got leukemia!" Sharon had collapsed on the basketball court while playing two nights before. At the hospital, the doctor's first test concluded that there was a ninety per cent chance that it was the dreaded fatal disease, called blood cancer or leukemia. For two weeks tests were run; and then, the results found that Sharon was the one person in ten who had a blood infection which could be cured - not leukemia.

For Victor Zeller's family, the ordeal - the state of siege was over. But, what about the families of the other nine, those who really had leukemia and died?

One study of forty such families revealed that the families where the children died, only one in ten remained intact. For seven out of the ten families, marital problems developed including many incidences of divorce. Many parents resorted to drinking.

Others required psychiatric care or developed a psychosomatic illness. Brothers and sisters of children who die with leukemia often have adjustment problems and school difficulties.

The families with the worst problems were those who refused to face up to the seriousness of the disease. Some would not allow themselves to cry or permit sadness, others tried to escape by changing jobs, buying a new house - or, in some cases, women in getting pregnant. These activities only added more stress. Some families, after death, enshrined the child's room. Others banned any mention of the child as if he or she never existed.

The families who coped best were those who were prepared for the worst - those who gave honest information to all family members including the patient. They expressed their sadness, their grief, and prepared for the death of that child.

We are always looking to the future - a vacation, the next promotion or retirement - and this is good. Yet,

the real problem is coping with today

its frustrations, its heartaches, its pains, its grief, and its loneliness.

There is no explanation for the untimely death of a loved one of any age, particularly a child. We should not be ignorant about death - we should be honest with ourselves and others. We should permit ourselves grief - to cry, and to express our emotions, for the temporary or eternal separation caused by death.

For those who die "in Christ," the body goes in the ground or is cremated. The soul instantly goes to be with Christ (Ref. 1). As Paul stated in Philippians 1:21, "For to me, to live is Christ and to die is gain." Those who have accepted Christ as their Savior will live in Christ on the Day of the Lord (Jesus second coming). "First, the Christian dead will rise; then, we who are left alive shall join them, caught up to meet the Lord.

⊚⊚

Thus, we shall always be
with the Lord"

⊚⊚

(1st Thessalonians 4:16b-18)

Sandra Kinner was seven when the car struck her. At the graveside service, the minister, Rev. Ben Haden, spoke with authority, "We come not to bury Sandra for Sandra isn't here. We come to bury the body in which her soul lived on earth. Sandra knew Christ. She is with him in heaven now. God selects the perfect time to be born, and the perfect time to die. Sandra cannot come back to join us. Sandra is one of our investments in heaven."

Sandra's earthly body, and ours, is just a temporary wrap around our eternal soul. Our entry into Heaven or Hell depends on whether or nor we have prayed to received Jesus as Savior and Lord.

When we have lost a close loved one, what do we say to the survivor? Some say, "Take a trip." Others say, "Keep busy or let me know if there is something I can do for you." The best thing often is to give the person a hug and say, "I love you!"

There is no mathematical proof - no scientific explanation. We know, on the basis of God's word and compelling evidence that Christ died and on the third day was resurrected. He appeared to over five hundred. He appeared to James and the other Apostles. He appeared to Paul on the road to Damascus via a sudden light and Jesus spoken words.

This is the Christian certainty: we trust in Christ alone for eternal life and not our good works. We will be together again - with those who died before us and those who die after us – in Heaven, in eternity with Christ (Ref. 2)

There will be no more pain or suffering anymore. Time will not exist. We will eternally worship the living God. And, it is certain that we will be with and know those who have gone before including Sandra.

You may be thinking about whether or not you're going to Heaven. If you were to die tonight, do you KNOW FOR CERTAIN that you will wake up in Heaven?

We can know for certain that you will wake up in Heaven when you die! If you would like to know for certain that you will wake up in Heaven, please read on!

Note 1: This chapter was written prior to the author's wife's death. Chapter 19, "She's Gone – Death of a Spouse" was written after her death.

Ref. 1: Barnhouse, Dr. Donald Grey, "Death Is Swallowed Up in Victory," Alliance of Confessing Evangelicals, Philadelphia, PA., www.AllianceNet.org.

Ref. 2: Jeremiah, Dr. David, "Where Are They Now?", Turning Point, San Diego, CA 92163, www.turningpointonline.org.

4 ON BEING AVERAGE!

"Do not be conformed to this world . . ."

Romans 12:2 a

CHAPTER FOUR

ON BEING AVERAGE!

"Do not be conformed to this world."

Romans 12:2

John Frazier was up at 6:00 a.m. as usual. Shaved and dressed for work, he sat down for breakfast with his wife, Anne, his daughter, Jill, age sixteen and son, Bill, age fourteen. The family atmosphere was very good - plans were made to go to the college football game Saturday afternoon. John loved college football and sometimes went to two games on a Saturday if schedules permitted.

John left for the factory office. He had just passed his forty-fifth birthday. For the past nine years, he had been the Assistant Department Manager of one of the sales departments. Everyone liked John. He was friendly and witty – a pleasure to be around. His boss was about his age. Always on time, capable and competent, John had moved up to middle management quickly.

Bill and Jill were off to school. Anne settled in with her morning chores, after a chat with one of her best friends on the phone - Betty White. Yes – John and Anne would certainly be at the bridge club that night and at the school PTA meeting the next night.

John usually arrived at work on time or early at Jolly Textiles. John's boss noted after 8:15 am that John had not come in on time, but no need for alarm. A little after nine, he phoned Anne to ask about John. This set in motion concern and anxiety.

John had never deviated more than a few minutes from his usual schedule without telling Anne. Both loved each other and their children. Their marriage had taken them through many good times over the past twenty years. As Anne hung up the phone, a City Police car pulled up in the driveway. A senior officer met Anne at the door. "Mrs. Frazier, can you please come to the hospital with me?"

"Why?" asked Anne!

Shortly before 8:00 am, a car had driven off the boat ramp into the lake at the Country Club where the Frazier's kept their sixteen foot ski boat. In shallow water, the car and body of the driver- (John Frazier) - were quickly recovered. "Why? . . . Why? . . .

◎◎

*Why? was the question
asked by all?"*

◎◎

A good job, a happy home, a frequent attendant at church, a member of the church's Board of Deacons – John had everything on earth - but he had taken his own life.

Frank Clark heard the news and shuddered. He was John's best friend for twenty years. They had started out in business together and had played golf together weekly. Though he and Jane spent much time with the Fraziers, (they attended the same Sunday School Class), they had never discussed Christ. Everyone assumed that because he went to church, he was a Christian. They had never prayed together.

Their Sunday School Class was often devoted to theological questions. Often, it ended with the class confused. Their church was growing - a new building was planned. Structure and administration took priority. As the membership grew, relationships and concern for human needs fell back in priority. Their attitude was money and maintenance over ministry and missions.

In looking back, John's friends could see signs they should have recognized. He had become more of a loner; he had dropped out of conversations. He had held back. John felt that he was a failure - he had no place to go in the firm. His boss was young and competent. His own chances of promotion were poor. His job was routine now, even boring. Living a surface existence - work, golf, bridge, and football games - life lost its meaning.

John had an excellent service record in the U. S. Air Force in World War II. He was a crew member on a C-46 flying supplies over the hump in Asia to support other troops. John was a loyal American and could not understand the changes and disintegration of integrity in the government of his country.

He felt like a misfit in a changing world. As his friends looked back, they should have realized that John clearly was becoming depressed, but they did not suspect the seriousness of his condition. He did not seek medical attention. Generally, depression can be treated successfully. His value system seemed to be fading away with nothing of substance to replace his ethical beliefs.

Many suicides occur in the age group of 45 to 54. At this time in life, a man sees a younger person moving up in his company. He realizes there are goals he will never reach. For women, middle age might be just as difficult. When the children leave home, the pattern of their lives may be broken. Both men and women may not be as physically attractive. They may feel useless.

We all want our lives to be meaningful. We do not want our lives to be as "footprints in the sand".

A fortieth or fiftieth birthday can sometimes be an ominous thing for the individual who takes time out to think. Youth is gone. The eagerness of anticipation is slowly giving way to mental recollection. It has been said, "Youth rides in the cab of the locomotive and jubilantly surveys the track ahead. Age rides in the caboose and gazes back with sweet sorrow, upon fading scenes of the past." It requires an adjustment.

At one time, Sweden. had the highest standard of living in the world. The country's socialistic form of government provided every need from the cradle to the grave. There was no poverty. Yet, this nation had the highest suicide rate of any country on earth. Denmark and Sweden may be the least religious nations on earth.

A recent survey (Ref. 1) indicated that Sweden was the least religious nation in the world with up to 85 percent atheist and agnostics. Sweden was followed by Vietnam, Denmark, Norway and Japan in the top five of ten nations listed.

Less than five percent may attend the state churches. Yet, these societies seem morally, stable, humane and good. When asked about death, one person stated, "I never really thought much about that." What happens to the Christian West when it ceases to be Christian" (Ref. 2)? Moralism is of little or no value when one is facing death or loss of a loved one, particularly from suicide.

Some suicides result from a sense of guilt, shame, or recollection of sin. Many persons sense of guilt or shame deepens by sermons from the pulpit and the "thou shalt not" philosophy.

Many can recite long passages from the Bible. Few can honestly understand the basic philosophy which they are reciting and few live in accordance with the rules being quoted.

Many go to church because it seems to be expected of them. It is a religious practice; it is a social habit. That's where their friends are. Sometimes, as one gazes across a congregation on a Sunday - the group assembled seems merely a group of parrots. They seem to be in a trance - often, not knowing the historical basis of their religion, nor caring deeply about what the minister may be saying.

The church, his family, his business, and John's friends had failed him. They had failed to teach John two things: (A) How to know for certain that you were going to Heaven when you die, and (B) What to say to God if asked: "Why should I let you into My Heaven?"

They had failed to place the emphasis sharing the Gospel with people, doing evangelism, on receiving Christ, of working to help others, and living in joyful expectation of an eternity with Christ. Life is just a breath when compared to eternity in heaven. Our goal is to be with Jesus - it is not: going up the organization, earthly pleasures or materialistic satisfactions.

Some academic and theological discussions serve a useful purpose. When these dialogues attacks the validity of the Bible, when they confuse those who are not so well educated, when they fail to build a wonderful basis for living - these methods must be suspect. Christianity is not a collective philosophy; it is all about an individual, personal relationship with Christ. By reading the Bible daily, by talking with Christ in prayer daily, by taking our problems, our frustrations, our anxieties and our boring jobs to Him - we can find comfort and hope in this world. We are not alone!

Try as we may to avoid the subject of death, death comes to all of us. Plan as we might, death may be just as near for the child as for the elderly person. Let's not waste a moment - let's tell the good news of Christ's dying for our sins, of Jesus conquering death - of faith, hope, love, and heaven. Let's not permit another death like John Frazier's to occur. Suicide is not the answer for a Christian.

For those who have accepted Christ, salvation is eternal. Therefore, suicide does not keep us out of Heaven.

☯☯

"The name of the Lord is a strong tower; The righteous run to it and are safe".

☯☯

Proverbs 18:10.

Let's keep our eye on the only valid target and live confidently and peacefully despite the accelerating pace of existence. Future shock may destroy the world, nuclear war may eradicate humanity, the stock market may crash, yet it will not be the end. It will reinforce the Christian looking forward to the return of Christ and being with Him in Heaven for eternity.

Reg. 1: Johnson, Gary, "The Johnsons in Sweden," April 16, 2009.

Ref. 2: Steinfels, Peter, "A land of Nonbelievers, Which Is Not to Say Atheist," NEW YORK TIMES, February 28, 2009, Page A15.

5 COST REDUCTION MANDATE

"Find your strength in the Lord. Stand your ground when things are at their worst."

Ephesians 6: 10-13

CHAPTER FIVE

COST REDUCTION MANDATE

"Find your strength in the Lord.
Stand your ground when
things are at their worst."

Ephesians 6: 10-13

As manager of manufacturing operations, Shirley Scott has spent a substantial part of her time building loyalty, confidence, and security with her people - department supervisors, foremen and employees at all levels. As Shirley moved up the management ranks herself, she worked to improve relations with the union, and in order to cultivate civic and public confidence in business.

Shirley's plant is a small division of a conglomerate business group. The major product of the corporation is knitted textiles. This product has come under pricing and cost pressure due to over-capacity in the industry, a shift in styling requirements plus a move to out source production to lower cost countries like Mexico and China. Though Shirley's Division was profitable, the total complex had shifted into a loss operation after years of profitability.

Management changed at the top. A new president was selected. He was a hard-nosed financially oriented man directed to reverse the financial fortunes of the firm. Then, improved economic conditions began to change the outlook

A management consulting firm was engaged to evaluate all operations. Regardless of efficiency of individual operations or departments, a ten per cent across-the-board reduction in personnel was ordered. The consultant, "Black Angel" as he is referred to by the firm's managers, quickly reviewed each person's job and decided who would be fired. An outsider, he had little knowledge of the firm, its people, or their concerns.

Even with the good financial results of Shirley's Division, she received instructions to comply with the ten per cent rule. Shirley objected, pointing out the reasons. Her union contract was under negotiation and a shortage of qualified people, particularly mechanics, had made hiring difficult.

Realizing her inability to fight the corporate hierarchy, Shirley agreed to the termination, but requested that she be given three to six months to let attrition take part of the toll, combine some jobs; and then terminate those remaining on a timely basis to allow them to find other employment, plus cushion the shock of being fired.

Nevertheless, the edict came down on a Wednesday: "Fire forty-three people Friday morning; have them out of the plant within thirty minutes of their being given termination notices. Give only the benefits required by government and company policy".

Shirley again objects and talks directly to the new president. Once again she explains the situation; but, the decision stands (to implement the terminations on Friday morning). "Don't you think this method is cruel", Shirley asks. "No," says her new boss, "just practical." With that finality, Shirley tells her key managers to report for an 8:00 am Friday meeting in her office.

She gives them the word, the party-line as to reasons, and asks that each person be informed immediately. She will talk with each individual employee.

One person has been in the Division only two years, but he has been with the present firm for twenty six years. "Why can I not be transferred back to my former job?" The answer was "No". "But, is this fair," he asked? Shirley can only answer, "Company policies say Division seniority is the controlling factor, not company service."

The employee had never sought another job. He had been very loyal to the firm. After twenty six years with one company, there was really no place for him to go. Finding a job in one's late forties is difficult, almost impossible in the fifty plus range.

After twenty-six years, he had thirty minutes to clean out his desk and get out. He could come back the next week to pick up his personal items. The company did not want him around creating friction or disturbing other employees for the rest of the day. He asked Shirley, "Why must I leave so quickly? I have been here twenty-six years. I am not a thief." Shirley had no answer.

Another employee said, "My wife is having a baby next month. "Can I just work until I find another job? It is far more difficult to find a job when I am unemployed rather than when I am still working." Again, the answer is, "No - you will have unemployment benefits."

A young, excellent cost accountant heard the news and said, "But, I gave up a good job to come here. You said I had a shot at the Controller's job. What have I done wrong? Is your word no good?" Shirley could simply say, "I'm sorry."

The job finished, Shirley never once, as a good manager, placed the blame on top management or the consultant. She headed home for lunch wondering,

◎◎
"Why, why must it be this way? Is it really worth it to be a manager?"
◎◎

She had spent years building a foundation of trust; then it was all gone. No one will believe her now. She is simply a pawn in the game of business. Frustrated at the little control she had over events, what is her response as a Christian manager?

Managers must build a secure environment within their firms, and their employees must know where they stand. The employees must have confidence in their managers, their businesses and their firms so that they can sleep at night without the worry of being fired the next day. Constant changes in management and in the direction of the existing firm erode the loyalty of the existing people and cause difficulty in attracting new personnel. Continuous changes in management and crash program cost reductions are not the answer.

Business managers and industries in the free enterprise system must build firms where people can work with security. Continuing personnel changes and cyclical terminations may lead to government legislation to prevent firing people unjustly.

Christian business managers should not take advantage of people. They should not institute personnel practices or take actions which will destroy loyalty, or confidence, and or a secure working environment. Christian business managers should not need government legislation to do what they should do themselves, for their businesses and/or their industries.

In some countries, it is very difficult to terminate an employee. In some situations, a year or more advanced pay - often two years - must be given to a person who is fired. In certain nations, a person is literally hired for life. Do we want the unethical practices of business managers to fuel the need for such legislation in North America or internationally? NO!

Yet, generalities do not solve Shirley Scott's problem. She still has the dilemma - she must go back to the plant Monday morning. Prayer is her only hope - to seek guidance from Christ.

Basically, every situation falls into three categories:

1. true and important,
2. true and trivial or
3. false.

❦

It is sorting out the true and important from the true and trivial situations that is difficult.

❦

Policies of management which are true and trivial can be tolerated or ignored. For those we consider true and important - and Shirley Scott's situation falls into this category - we have two choices:

1. change the policy by working from within or
2. if this fails, get out.

Sometimes, it seems from the outside that the person in Shirley's position should be able to change the organization. Yet, in many cases, it is not possible for middle managers, such as Shirley, to reverse the direction of higher management. We cannot live in an organization with such cancerous conduct.

A firm is no better than its leaders. An old Finnish fish proverb says, "Wherever the head goes, the tail will surely follow." Very frequently, firms have personalities - often similar to the personality of their leader or leaders. People will probably be attracted to the organization if they have similar personalities, modes of conduct and ethical beliefs as the leader.

An Englishman, C. Northcote Parkinson, wrote a book, Parkinson Law, on corporations. He stated, "higher officials are plodding and dull, those less senior are active in intrigue against each other, and the junior managers are frustrated" (Ref. 1). This is the situation at Shirley's firm causing the need to bring in a consultant.

As a manager, we must always take action.

Indecision is the greatest problem in business.

If a manager takes a decision and it is wrong; then, the matter can be corrected. A good rule is to aim for the top of the highest mountain and you will surely achieve a high hill. Aim for the gutter and you will surely get there.

To be a successful or winning manage is difficult. You will be lonely (but not alone) often and sometimes frightened. Many students of management believe that successful management is some mystic intuition given to only a few. Successful management remains doing simple things over and over and paying attention to details day after day.

Shirley Scott - and all managers - must make every effort to change their firms from the inside. If Shirley cannot change the basic unethical practices of her firm from within, she must seek a new job for herself in another firm. Constant compromise of her ethical beliefs will result in the deterioration of her moral standards and her personal unhappiness.

The most effective managers are those who maintain low cost operations continuously. Cost reductions will be made when times are good and employees can find other jobs. In economic downturns, few layoffs would be necessary. Short work weeks and rotating weeks off permit loyal, critical personnel to stay on the job with benefits. There is never a need for a "Black Angel" in well managed firms.

Ref. 1: Boice, James Montgomery, Philippians, Baker Books, Grand Rapids, MI, Fourth Printing, 2000, Page 80.

6 THE CRISIS AHEAD

"The gifts we possess differ as they are allocated by God's grace. Exercise your gift of management by managing. If you are a leader, exert yourself to lead and direct cheerfully."

Romans 12:6a-8b Paraphrased

CHAPTER SIX

THE CRISIS AHEAD

"The gifts we possess differ as they are allocated by God's grace. Exercise your gift of management in managing. If you are a leader, exert yourself to lead and direct cheerfully."

Romans 12: 6a-8b, Paraphrased

The Board expects a twenty per cent return on gross investment. The President expects a ten per cent increase in sales. Personnel in all jobs expect a five per cent wage increase.

Jim Hunt, Division President of the Solvent Division sits down one morning just to list all the things expected of him - by management, by customers, by employees - and the list is formidable.

As Jim scanned his computer screen, the stock market was taking a dive. His 401K retirement account was declining along with his personal investments. Jim was heavily invested in more risky stocks looking for a large gain.

But, bonds and more conservative investments were what he needed.

It seemed to Jim that his job consisted of one crisis after another.

☯☯

Who would walk through the door next with some disrupting situation?

☯☯

Jim had spent over ten years in the industrial chemical business, working his way up. He knew the business inside and out. He had just been on a sales trip with his Vice President of Sales to the West Coast. Yes - sales were good and no serious problems existed in the Western region. But, how long would that last before a competitor came in with a lower price, a better product?

How long would it be before the friction which existed between the Vice President of Sales and the Vice President of Product Development erupted into the open? Could he keep the lid on the Division long enough to get that next promotion? His wife expected it! Jim couldn't help but wonder, "Is the continuing struggle worth it"?

"How was my day? I will tell you how was my day. An unending succession of business triumphs, heartwarming personal encounters, frequent compliments, lavish bonuses and stock market killings beyond my wildest dreams. How was your day?

The true and important question Jim and all Christian managers must ask is, "What does God/Jesus expect?" This is the key to competent management

The task of our age is to translate the individual ethic, "Love thy neighbor as thyself," into a corporate expression. Tensions must be replaced with genuine concern. The vast majority of our employees are honest and want to do a good job - to have secure employment and confidence about the future. Management must provide the opportunity.

When we quit working for the Board, for Management, for the next promotion - when we start working for God after we have bowed in submission to Christ; He is waiting to reinforce us with creative inspiration and forgiving grace. When we start working with Him, doing what He wants us to do, confidence will replace frustration and peace will replace anxiety.

When we respond to Him by being totally honest, totally truthful, morally disciplined with heartfelt compassion demonstrated in our own character and behavior; then, this atmosphere may begin to spread throughout the firm, from the factory floor and to the Board room.

It is not our policies or directives which get results. It is not overworked terms, such as, "worldview", computer science or knowledge management that form the basis for manage-

ment. It is our people working together, to contribute their lives to a meaningful purpose and
a useful business.

There is a seed built into every person - a seed
waiting to germinate, a talent waiting to be un-
covered, a need waiting to be filled, and a hurt
waiting to be understood. Job enrichment is
not a systematic personnel program. It is recognition, as a person, an individual human rather
than an employee number on a computer record. This is what God expects us to strive for,
and to build a creative business environment of
love, security and care for our customers, our
coworkers, and our stockholders.

☙❧

*The character of a business starts
at the top.*

☙❧

The Division will be a reflection of Jim.
When the door is open for Christ to come into
his heart, a manager finest hour will be ahead -
at work, at home, and in eternity.

For fifteen or more years, (of over forty years
in business) I worked with firms in trouble in
various parts of the world - turnaround management. In the vast majority of cases, the significant problem was management. In only

one assignment were the people on the factory floor the problem (which eventually resulted in a plant closure). And, those people were being encouraged to go the wrong way by union leaders.

Listen . . . are you listening? The world of business remains the greatest mission field on earth, an opportunity to witness for Christ. We are not alone!

7 BIBLE-TOTING BUSINESSMAN

"Show yourself guileless and above reproach, faultless children of God in a warped and crooked generation in which you shine like stars in a dark world...."

Philippians 2:14-15a

CHAPTER SEVEN

BIBLE TOTING BUSINESSMAN

"Show yourself guileless and above reproach, faultless children of God in a warped and crooked generation, in which you shine like stars in a dark world...."

Philippians 2:14-15a

❧❧

"If I ever see another businessman toting a Bible, I'm going to get up and run,"

❧❧

said Ben Winters to a group at dinner one evening in Oklahoma City.

What brought on this startling statement? Ben Winters was an employee of Godfrey Industries. Bill Godfrey was a young man in his early thirties, a dedicated Christian who sometimes spoke from the pulpit. In a humanitarian effort to help the Native Americans (Indians) in the

Oklahoma area, he had started Godfrey Industries, Inc.

The firm was originally a small shop fabricating children's clothes. Grants were available from the government to aid minorities. The business's growth was phenomenal. Soon, additional plants were being constructed and national recognition was achieved. An article in the Readers Digest recorded his achievements.

The glamour of success sent Bill Godfrey and his management team into other businesses - nursing homes, retail stores, and others businesses in which they had neither experience nor knowledge. With a Bible in his hand and prayer at every meeting, there seemed to be nothing but success in Godfrey Industries business ventures.

During the peak of one economic expansion and the height of Godfrey Industries' success, Bill Godfrey was making some one hundred to two hundred speeches annually. His company planes including one executive jet whisked him from one engagement to another.

Utilizing government grants, industrial development loans, and factoring accounts receivable - Bill Godfrey owned the majority of the stock with little actual cash investment. As material prices increased rapidly, the firm built inventories and profits grew fictitiously through inventory write-ups.

The stock market was right, and Bill Godfrey went public with Godfrey Industries, Inc. He put aside a substantial portion of the money received by selling stock to the innocent public for his own personal needs and those of his family by placing his assets in his wife's name free of encroachment in the event of business disaster.

The company provided cars for him and his family. His company's credit cards, among other things, clothed his wife and children. He rationalized using his credit card in this way as his wife required clothes for business and public functions in the company's interest. Many personal costs were classified as business expenses. This sort of greed and tax manipulation became a way of life for Bill and Godfrey Industries.

Then, Bill Godfrey's empire began tumbling down. The economic slowdown and reduced raw material prices caused large business losses and plus values of inventories to decline. Factory expansions begun at the wrong time were completed causing large idle capacity losses.

The banks began to take over, and influence management decisions. The company's Aircraft Division was eliminated, one plant was closed, and then another; until three-fourths of the firm's employees were unemployed. Finally, Godfrey Industries' stock was de-listed from the NASDAQ exchange.

Private investors, company employees and others who had purchased stock at up to $25.00 per share had worthless paper on their hands. Chapter 11 bankruptcy was declared. Under Chapter 11, the courts appointed an administrator of Godfrey Industries. Bill Godfrey declared personal bankruptcy - but, he was safe. His assets had cleverly been placed in the names of his wife and family, not Godfrey Industries, Inc.

Having a Bible on our desk and speaking in churches does not make one a Christian. A personal relationship with Christ and Bill's conduct were not compatible. The power of greed overwhelmed Bill. Despite these faults, Bill may well have repented and received his eternal salvation from Christ.

Somewhere between Godfrey's ambitions and his ideals, his ethical compass went astray. Though we must constantly be in prayer, ever, ready to find direction from God, prayer is no substitute for poor performance on our part. We cannot lay the blame on God when we fail.

Christian businessmen and businesswomen - more than others - must do an excellent job and be a good example in their personal and business conduct. They must be professional managers, capable and well-qualified. Management is a constant learning experience. Also, it is essential that calm and sound decisions be made. The firm must achieve security and stability in order to develop a lasting business, a model for others to follow, a contribution to society as well as business achievement.

It is very satisfactory for a Christian to have good earnings even large sums. Yet, the money must be:

(1) earned honestly,
(2) spend adequate time with their family and children,
(3) give a tithe to their church and
(4) missionaries and other Christian ministries.

When Christian businessmen do not have sound financial systems, when their cash resources are stretched too far, when they operate their businesses based on feeling rather than professional management; then, failure is not God's fault. When we make simple mistakes, when we fail to apply common sense and fail to be professional in our management practices, we cannot expect to throw out the lifeline of prayer in desperation to save our careers or business. Yet, God is always ready to listen to our prayers and guide us in the right direction.

Even in failure, we can sincerely accept Christ and the eternal salvation he offers everyone!

⊚⊚

Jesus is for winners and losers.

⊚⊚

Some people have to become losers before they get enough wisdom to be eternal winners. A good example of this fact is Chuck Colson who served time in prison for Watergate and his Prison Fellowship (Ref. 1).

Ref. 1: Colson, Chuck, Prison Fellowship, PrisonFellowship.org.

8 THE AGE OF GREED

"If you go on fighting one another, tooth and nail, all you can expect is mutual destruction."

Galatians 5:15

CHAPTER EIGHT

<u>THE AGE OF GREED</u>

"If you go on fighting one another, tooth and nail, all you can expect is mutual destruction."

Galatians 5:15

Integrity . . . Integrity in times like these?

"What's in it for me responds Bill Wilson as his boss suggests that he take on another assignment. After all, Harry Stevens got a raise last week and he just stays in the same job.

A strange quiet often exists in the office, when the battle lines are drawn between people. A phony atmosphere in the management meeting may be covering up the battle for more money, a promotion, a company car, or a bigger office.

❦

*In many ways, company "politics"
is a more difficult challenge.*

❦

It is more complicated. It divides people rather than uniting them. Company politics can become war with a tongue and war with action, rather than with physical weapons. Gossip in the office can be more deadly than gossip at the bridge club.

Over three-fourths of our people today do not know what hard times are - few lived through the great depression. Most do not have memories of World War II. The younger workers have no personal experience with un-employment.

❦

*Practically all have been brought
up in a home of plenty, a world
of affluence, with often too much
stuff.*

❦

Our college trainees think they should receive large salaries, guaranteed bonuses, luxury offices, the latest computers and communications devices, not to mention a parking space. It may never have occurred to them that in years past a college education was something one had to work to obtain. They do not understand that one group cannot get more from the company than another, and that a person must give more than he receives.

In most of the advanced societies, the old disciplines of unemployment and grinding poverty have largely disappeared. We never wish to see them return. The problem is what to put in their place, for no free society can exist without its proper disciplines.

Toynbee, the English historian, packing his bags in London to retire on his son's Yorkshire farm, commented with gloom, "I feel there is something incorrigible about us, a selfishness here in this island, and a scramble for all among the nations, each looking out for itself. We are measuring everything by money. The irony of it is that even our money is melting away."

Even our Money is Melting Away

In business, it sometimes seems like an Age of Greed - every person working for himself, a selfishness, a scramble for the top by everyone.

No free society, no company or group can exist without discipline, without absolutes. The dilemma cannot be solved by changing collective groups - it can only be solved by individual Biblical morality.

"What's in it for me?" must be changed to, "What can I do to help?" Strength may not be in one's position or the authority to hire or fire a person. Christian kindness is not a sign of weakness. Forgiving infinitely more than we are forgiven is following the instructions of Christ to forgive not "seven times but seventy times seven."

An Age of Greed expresses itself in many ways. It may be the secretary using the company copy machine for a club project, the worker taking home a roll of tape, the executive mailing his personal letters in the company mail room, the salesman's wife using the company car to run an errand and in many other ways.

Little things, such as these, are the cells which grow into a cancer of dishonesty and selfishness.

⌘

The devil is alive and well in the world of business, giving silent encouragement to steal, to cheat on taxes, and to be greedy.

⌘

Everything in the world goes full circle. What we do unto others, they will probably do unto us.

Jesus taught us to, "Do unto others as you would have them do unto you." When we take advantage of others, our time will come. When we cheat or steal, in both LITTLE THINGS and big ones, the day of reckoning is not too far ahead. When we are dishonest or tell half truths to achieve a goal - it is sin, it is wrong-doing. "Do not steal" covers more than taking money.

George Wells was the owner of one of the firms for which I did consulting work. The business was very profitable – one of the top three - maybe the top earner in that industry. The company had just finished an excellent year – higher sales, higher profits. In reviewing the financial results, George said, "What can we do to increase profit in the New Year?" I said, "George – the company has had a great year, how much is enough." He answered, "It really does not matter, it is just the way we keep score in business."

A baseball player obtains a long term contract for $25-million per year. An executive who receives $250-million to take over a big business, and drive it into the ground, and close stores, and fire people, is fired and takes home his bonus worth millions of dollars (golden parachute) is a selfish, greedy executive. Amazingly, he is hired by another high profile firm.

An investment firm writes off billions in loan losses, and the Chief Executive has a salary of $84-million not to mention benefits as well as the company Gulfstream V Jet. Then, the business must be sold due to lack of sufficient capital.

An investment firm goes bankrupt as a result of bad management and excessively risky loans. Its stockholders and its debt holders have billions in losses. The chief executive is fired and takes home a $22-million retirement package while thousands of employees are terminated with little severance pay or benefits. The executive has been paid nearly a half-billion dollars from 1993 to 2007 (Ref. 1).

☙❧

How much is enough?

☙❧

Christ can give us the strength to overcome these temptations, to overcome the devil in the office. Jesus said, "Resist the devil and he will flee from you." All we have to do is let Him walk with us day by day, and put our hand in His hand, as we walk through an Age of Greed. Then, we will know when enough is enough. Biblical principles and God's guidance will show us when enough is enough. We never need walk alone!

Integrity . . . Integrity in times like theses? Yes!

Ref. 1: Kristof, Nicholas D., "Need a Job? $17,000 an Hour, No Success Required," NEW YORK TIMES, September 18, 2008, Page A33

9 NEW MAN FROM THE OUTSIDE

"Therefore, be merciful, just as your Father is merciful."

Luke 6:36

CHAPTER NINE

NEW MAN FROM THE OUTSIDE

"Therefore, be merciful, just as your
Father is merciful."

Luke 6:36

For Marion Bellyard, the time had arrived.
For twenty years he had been employed by
National Building Products. He had worked
his way up to Vice President of Manufacturing
over the past eighteen years. As a member of
the Executive Group for over five years, he had
been aiming for the position of President.

Now, the existing President was taking early
retirement at the age of sixty-two. The other
executives on the scene were younger than him
and lacked the necessary seniority in the company. The Board was to meet at 2:00 p. m. that
day.

He had thought it all out in his mind. As
soon as the Board called him and offered him
the job as President, he would ring his wife and
they would have a celebration. He had told his

wife about the situation and she, too, confidently expected that he would be appointed. So it was with much excitement that he went to the office that morning.

The Chairman had been in the preceding morning to talk with him, review his record with the firm, and everything seemed to be in order. As he went by his secretary's desk that morning, she said, "Mr. Callahan (the Chairman) would like to see you when you have a few minutes." His heart jumped with excitement - maybe they had already made up their minds. Maybe, they would tell him now.

Since an open door policy existed and he knew the Chairman well, Marion walked into the office confidently expecting the promotion to President. But, the Chairman began on a different track. He began to point out that the company was sales and marketing oriented; that the company had not grown as fast as it should; that the profits were not at the level which they desired; and, that they needed a man knowledgeable in all aspects of the business– particularly marketing - to give it a new direction that it required.

Marion began to become a bit uneasy. The Chairman pointed out that the Manufacturing Division was the best Division in the firm. The costs were low and competitive. Personnel morale was excellent; quality was under good control; and, capital investments had paid off and technology was current. He complimented Marion in every way he could.

Then, the thunderbolt struck! He said, "We have decided to bring in a new man from the outside to give our company the new direction we need plus the strength required in sales and marketing."

Marion could not believe it. His resentment, anger, frustration, and disappointment were plainly obvious. He pointed out to the Chairman that he certainly was disappointed, but that he would work with the new man in every way practical.

As the days passed, the resentment and disappointment increased. At one point, Marion considered resigning. He even considered taking his own life.

About one month later, Jerry Fields arrived to take over the President's office. He called the Management Team together and asked for their help. He pointed out that he could not do the job alone; that every executive would be retained and that the characteristics of the old firm would be maintained. He said that no one should rock the boat and that the necessary changes would take place gradually in line with the objectives of the previous President.

But, the disappointment in Marion had not subsided.

❦❦

He knew the games that people
could play in management, and
he would play his game, too.

❦❦

Outwardly, he would support the new President; but behind the scenes, - he would work for his immediate downfall so that the job would open up again and give him another chance at President.

As a Christian, he knew that this backstabbing was wrong. With much prayer and much soul searching, Marion decided that he would not play that game. He would help the new President succeed.

As the months began to pass, Marion observed Jerry in every detail. He began to see that he was honest, sincere, and working to make National Building Products a better company. Marion also began to see that he was bringing in new products, new ideas and that the company was prospering. Further, it was obvious that Jerry was making an effort to broaden Marion's background and experience. He sent him to Harvard Business School's course in Marketing. He broadened his area of responsibility.

Then, Jerry had a heart-to-heart talk with Marion. He said, "I know you are disappointed.

Mr. Callahan told me you were next in line for the job of President. I want you to know I'm going to make every effort to see that you get it next. I don't believe in a President staying in a job more than five years. As soon as you are ready, I will move out."

Marion began to see that he wasn't really qualified when the job had become open earlier. He began to see that he was not a salesman; he was not knowledgeable in advertising and product promotions. But, he was capable of learning and Jerry was giving him the chance. He was careful to note in the Management Meeting with the Chairman and in the Board Meetings that Jerry always took the responsibility for anything that went wrong.

No matter who was at fault, Jerry accepted the responsibility. And, Jerry never took credit for success. He always gave credit for any of the achievements of the firm to the appropriate executive or other person at any level in the company.

Three years later, Jerry called Marion in and advised him that he was being promoted to Executive Vice President. From here on, he would be responsible for all operations including sales and marketing.

Jerry confided in Marion telling him that he (Jerry) had a shot at being President of one of the other larger Divisions. The only qualification was that he had to leave the President of the existing Division in good hands with capable management. He told Marion that he needed him to take over the job as quickly as possible. Within six months, Jerry had moved up and Marion was now President.

As he looked back, as he was a success in his new job - he could easily see what he could not understand before. Had he been promoted at the earlier time, he would have failed. He did not know enough about sales and marketing. His experience was not broad enough in depth and scope. He had not been prepared to take over the company at that difficult time.

Now, he was ready.

❦❦

"Those who wait on the Lord shall renew their strength;

❦❦

They shall mount up with wings like eagles, They shall run and not be weary. They shall walk and not faint.", Isaiah 40:31

10 IT DIDN'T HAVE TO BE THAT WAY

"It will be harder for a rich man to enter the Kingdom of Heaven than for a camel to pass through the eye of a needle."

Matthew 19:24

CHAPTER TEN

IT DIDN'T HAVE TO BE THAT WAY

"It will be harder for a rich man to
enter the Kingdom of Heaven than
for a camel to pass through the
eye of a needle."

Matthew 19:24

With all the glitter he had spent his life trying
to avoid, Peter Rains was buried. The church
where the funeral service was held contained as
many dazzling women as a gala movie opening.
Miss Wells, a beauty queen, sat weeping on the
front row pew. Flowers were everywhere. Social-
ite friends mingled with famous persons. Eulo-
gies were delivered. Peter was only thirty-five
when he died. The minister said, "It is not how
long we live, but what we do with our lives that
matters."

Television and movie cameras recorded
the event. Police were needed to control the
traffic.

◎◎

At the funeral, Peter's friends
were "going through the motions."

◎◎

A week earlier, Peter was rounding a curve on a high speed race track. A mechanical fault developed in his race car. Peter was killed on impact when his car hit a barrier.

The "Jet-set Playboy" and beneficiary to a fortune had spent his life trying to achieve, to find an individual identity. Told that he was born with a silver spoon in his mouth, he said, "Yes - but at the age of twenty-one, I pulled it out."

Winning was everything to Peter. He once said, "I'm going to lose the race. And that's as bad as anything I can visualize. To fail to win is the most painful thing imaginable. It (winning) is the thing I relate to most; the only thing I see as relevant."

Peter had all the money he could ever use, and scores of beautiful women flocked after him. He had the time and money to pursue any lifestyle that suited his fancy. But, none of this brought him the complete satisfaction for which he seemed to be searching. He (in his own words) did not want to "be alone in his room."

Good looking, affluent, Peter personified the man who had everything except perhaps the one thing he wanted most - inner, deep down peace in himself. It didn't have to be that way!

Many years later, Peter's family sold his accumulated memorabilia. Grown men wept as the auctioneer took bids on his high school letter, his rookie race driver's contract and photographs.

Man, by his very nature, must have a purpose in life; an attainable and satisfying purpose. The tortures of real hell are not only in the core of the earth, but in the very core of life. Here, too, is as close as we can get to heaven on earth as we look forward to the real Heaven in eternity with Christ. And in that vast gap in between, populated by those who have found neither overwhelming torture nor profound contentment - the lost souls are ambling without purpose during their allotted time on earth.

The great trouble with modern man is the unfortunate fact that he has no need for God. He envisions himself as the unquestioned center of life's drama, with the entire world a stage.

It is not necessary to wait a thousand years for a cure. Simple humility should be within the grasp of any who will make the effort to reach for it. Simple contentment is the reward for those who can look on life and find it good.

Satisfaction may be in losing honestly rather than winning dishonestly, in being off-stage rather then being on stage, by being a supporting helper to others on stage rather than by being the star of the show ourselves.

A client sold his business after 25 plus years of managing the operations to nearly a billion dollars in sales. His father had left two-thirds of the business to the son who managed it to success, James Hunter. The other third was left to the other younger son, Homer, who was successful on his own. When the $300-million received for the business was divided, James received $200-million and Homer $100-million. Homer called James and complained that the distribution was not fair. James replied, "You started with nothing and now you have $100-million. How much is enough." What will more millions bring us if the Lord were to ask, "Why should I admit you to my Heaven?" and finally realize that all the money on earth will not purchase a place in Heaven for anyone.

Five minutes of honest relaxation playing with a kitten and a piece of string can be better therapy than a frantic trip around the race track, in an effort to beat the flag, to win to increase earnings. At some point, we have to be satisfied with things as they are, not necessarily the way we want them to be for us.

But, in the stepped up tempo of modern life, it is amazing how few feel we can't afford to spend five minutes in such a trivial occupation – playing with a kitten, a dog, or smelling the roses.

The vacuum which existed in Peter's life is similar to that of many people - in business, at home being a housewife, in any mode of life.

◎◎

We have everything, yet nothing.

◎◎

Some people have periods of depression for lack of a whole life, for lack of a purpose, for lack of a meaning to life. We are always seeking to achieve, to climb an unseen mountain, and never know when the top has been reached. Could it be a misplacement of priority - a lack of finding the eye of the needle which leads to heaven with Christ on earth as well as in eternity? (Mathew 19:24)

◎◎

The man with millions of dollars struggles as hard and grubs as deep as does the man who is penniless.

◎◎

Yet, we do him an injustice to just interpret this as greed. It is commendable for a person to work. So long as he lives, he needs a purpose. He needs a challenge to his intellect and a spur to his ambition. The pursuit of dollars or fame is the only purpose he may have ever learned or can recognize.

None of this would be harmful in itself if the final reward was satisfying and eternal. But, unfortunately - it too often fails in the final test of satisfaction and it is only temporary.

The simple, basic and inescapable truth is that fear is multiplied rather than diminished by the acquisition of wealth or the attainment of fame. The more a man has to lose, the more he has to fear. Too much fear is a hazard to mental, physical and spiritual health.

If establishing financial wealth or a higher standard of living is a worthy goal, we must inevitably lose the very things we set out to gain. In acquiring new wealth, we acquire new fears. We acquire, also, a greater dependence on others whose services we are able to hire. We confine ourselves within a tightening cocoon of inhibitions. We lose physical, social, and psychological independence in the pursuit of financial independence, worldly fame, or fortune.

We do not have to be ever searching, alone in our room, alone in our office, alone in our race car, alone in our kitchen, alone at our school or

alone in our peer group. If Christ is with us –
in our minds, in our hearts – we will never be
alone!

Winning is something, but Jesus is everything
(Ref. 1).

Ref.1 Womack, Rusty, "Winning Is Something, but
Jesus Is Everything," Rehoboth Baptist Church, Tucker,
GA, February 1, 2009.

11 TAX LOOPHOLES

"Then He (Jesus) said to them, 'Give to Caesar what is Caesar's, and to God what is God's."

Mathew 22:21b

CHAPTER ELEVEN

TAX LOOPHOLES

"Then, He (Jesus) said to them,
'Give to Caesar what is Caesar's,
and to God what is God."

Mathew 22:21b

Bill Williams came into the living room shortly after dinner and asked, "Dad, can I have the car tonight?" His father passed him the keys and Bill drove off in the Ford Explorer to take his date to dinner and a movie approximately sixty miles away in Atlanta.

On the surface, this seems like a normal happening. The flaw is below the surface. The car was a company vehicle being depreciated on his father's books. The gas was charged on his father's company credit card and all expenses including dinner were paid by the firm.

The cost of the trip to Atlanta and back could have been credited back to the company. True, it would involve only a small cost of about $200 dollars. But, Bill's dad was a top level executive.

The expense was a significant gain to him for he did not pay income taxes on it as earned income.

How often do business people stretch the rules and charge personal expenses to the company? By almost any standard, this practice is stealing.

On Tuesday night, Katherine Lane phoned home from Durham, North Carolina. She told her mother that she would like to come home for the weekend, and her mother quickly replied, "I'll talk to your father about it. Possibly he can send the company plane."

On Friday afternoon, the company plane landed at Durham airport. About an hour and a half later–Katherine was home. The plane repeated the trip on Sunday afternoon. Katherine could have come by commercial plane. But the schedules were not very convenient, particularly the return trip on Sunday.

The company plane was a Beechcraft King Air. The estimated operating cost well over a thousand dollars per hour, or at least that would be the cost of leasing a plane for a similar trip. A total of six hours flying time was involved with a total cost to the company employing Katherine's father $7,500 or more.

The myth was in the plane's travel records. True, the pilot recorded all the data required by the FAA. But, the transportation department recorded both trips as business for Katherine's father.

Approximately $7,500 or more of the firm's money was expended which would not show up in profit for the public shareholders. Also, the government lost an opportunity to collect taxes on this corporate profit and the executive's personal income tax.

James Gibbs and his wife Mary were having a good time planning their trip to Las Vegas. On the surface, it seemed all right. The annual industry convention was being held in Las Vegas.

But, why Las Vegas, Nevada? After all, none of the industries' manufacturing plants or offices were located anywhere near Las Vegas. It was a long plane trip for people on the east coast which was where the majority of the industry association's members were located.

A close look at the program indicated a few business meetings each day. The majority of the time was spent on social occasions, golf and entertainment.

A package tour had been arranged by the industry association. They would board their chartered jet, all charges for plane fares, rooms and meals would be sent as an invoice from the industry association. Back home on the accounting books, one entry would show as travel expense for James. There would be no record that his wife went along nor that most of his time was spent on the golf course.

ᴏᴏ

Greed is ever present.

ᴏᴏ

Some hedge fund managers are making hundred of millions, even over a billion dollars a year. Some executive are paid tens or hundreds of millions of dollars including stock options and other benefits. Some top managers receive golden parachutes of tens of millions of dollars even for businesses that fail. How much is enough? How many people bought things for themselves or stuff for their children on credit cards?

In the recent financial turmoil and the housing bubble, many people obtained loans with little or no credit check and monthly payments they could not afford. Where were all the executives managing these businesses? It is almost as if they were blinded all around the world. Even a fool knew that firms advertising $500,000 loans at 3.5 percent interest rates with no credit check were stupid. Is God telling us something?

It is not more regulation which is needed. The Federal Reserve and our government cannot solve the problem. What we need is more integrity by individuals which will lead to ethical business operations and the elimination of financial turmoil.

Company cars, company planes, and industry conventions, are just some of the tax loopholes which exist for those who wish to take advantage of these temptations. Much is written about the morality of business, the ethics of business, and corruption in the world of business.

Reading about business scandals, millions of Americans are eager to believe that business behavior is getting worse. Others say that it is no worse than it always has been. Neither is correct and none can be proven. The Bible, God's word, tells us that times will get worse (lies, greed, divorce, violence, homosexuality and others) until Jesus returns.

Some writers point out those broad moral principles of society and ethical guidelines need to be revised with the acceleration of technology, the computer and the multi-national corporation. The question, "Is business morality adequate for today or tomorrow? The answer is NO."

The important question we should ask is, "How can business morality be improved?" Articles in most business publications tend to concentrate on management and business as a group.

❧❧

Yet, trying to improve business morality without changing individual morality is insane.

❧❧

The way to improve business morality is to begin work on ourselves, each of us as an individual.

The opportunity to cheat, to steal - in little things and big things - is ever present in the world of business. Some are legal - some are illegal. As Dr. D. James Kennedy asked in one sermon,

❧❧

"What is the going price of our soul?"

❧❧

The need for individual morality does not change with changing technology, changing markets and changing competition. Individual morality of truth and honesty transcend legal requirements or governmental legislation.

One need only go to the Bible to find the foundation for morality and for the ethics of business at any level. The standard has been set by Jesus in the Bible. We need only compare ourselves to it by asking the question when confronted with any decision, when challenged by any temptation, or any opportunity to lie, or cheat, or steal, or be dishonest, or utilize half truths. The question we need to ask ourselves is, "If Christ were here, what would He do?"

All of us are sinners. We all are estranged from God. Our hearts, minds, and deeds were once evil. But, now, by Christ's death - He offers us reconciliation to himself so that we may present ourselves before Him without blemish and innocent in His sight.

The only requirement is to die to selfish living and be born again with faith in Christ who said, "I am the way and the truth and the life. No one comes to the Father except through me." John 14:6. Then, our Father will blot out our sins and place our name in the Book of Life.

The need is to have Christ in us, in our hearts, in our minds, and in our actions. We need only look upon ourselves as a "representatives for Christ on earth," in faith and with the certain promise of glory to come for believers who have accepted His eternal salvation and eternal life.

12 EDUCATION DOESN'T MAKE YOU ANY SMARTER

"We know that we all possess knowledge. Knowledge puffs up, but love builds up. The man who thinks he knows something does not yet know as he ought to know."

I Corinthians 8: 1b-2

CHAPTER TWELVE

EDUCATION DOESN'T MAKE YOU ANY SMARTER

"We know that we all possess knowledge. Knowledge puffs up, love builds up. The man who things he knows something does not yet know as he ought to know."

I Corinthians 8: 1b-2

"I could not stand to take a cruise on a ship for a few days or a week. I could not imagine being cooped up on a cruise ship for a week with any group. I can't stand most people more than two hours." These are the statements of Billy Bonds.

Billy was an acknowledged authority in his field. With Ph.Ds in mathematics and aerospace, he was a recognized authority, a leading teacher and a sought after expert throughout the world.

To Billy, his life was education and knowledge. His children did not attend public schools. They were sent to private schools where they could get a better education. Isolated in their environment there, they could not associate or relate either to the needs of people or to the necessity of tolerance for others in person-to-person relationships. With Billy's wealth, the children had too much stuff and everything they could ever want without working for it or being responsible for much.

✿

"No" was not in the vocabulary of their parents.

✿

Billy was a theologian, too, or so he thought. He could quote the Bible at length and read the deepest, most complex theological books. As a Sunday school teacher, he often commented, "Anyone who believes the Bible literally may just as well leave this class now."

Each year our colleges turn out more graduates. Every year, the plaques on the wall multiply. The printing presses continue to turn out more books and publications than one could possibly master even if a single precisely defined subject is selected.

Authors of some management books concentrate on "knowledge" management. Governments want more "knowledge" or skilled industries in order to increase the value added.

Sometimes we tend to think that a college degree will solve our problems.

୧୨

We think that if mankind could just be educated, the world would be a better place.

୧୨

As one proceeds through the educational process, the knowledge process, there are three steps. The first step is one of AWE. There is so much to learn. Can we possibly ever know enough? The second step is CONFIDENCE. After mastering the computer, mathematics and science, one becomes self-confident and self-satisfied.

The financial crisis of 2008 is an example for all of us. The most brilliant people and managers all over the world could be in the banking and investment sector. Leaders of the central banks possess Ph.Ds and other advanced degrees.

Investment managers and bankers earned millions, even hundreds of millions of dollars, due to their academic background and business track record.

So, how did all these learned people all over the world fail to see the financial risk developing? How did they develop new financial instruments and let them explode out of control?

Nothing proved to be more dangerous and out of control than derivatives and credit default swaps. In 2002, the credit default swaps market was near $100-trillion. In only six years till 2008, the volume increased to over $500-trillion.

Warren E. Buffet described derivatives as, "financial weapons of mass destruction." "Theoretically intended to limit risk and ward off financial problems, the contracts instead have stoked uncertainty and actually spread risk amid doubts about how companies value them" (Ref. 1).

Where were all the diplomas and knowledge managers? A few questioned Federal Reserve Chairman, Alan Greenspan, but they were pushed aside. Where was Congress? Were the brilliant minds of all those in authority blinded?

Did greed overwhelm their analytical decision making?

The result was huge losses for just about everyone with the exception of those who actually caused the problem and could have prevented the crisis?

The third step is one of HUMBLENESS. We know so much, but the world is such a complex place. If our world tilted slightly, it would burn up. If the orbit varied just a tiny amount, we would not have the precise timing to maintain life. If we go a mere few thousand feet off the surface of the earth, life cannot be sustained without additional oxygen. God created the earth and life on it.

The more one learns, the more we realize the minuteness of man's knowledge, of man's achievements relative to the mightiness of the earth's systems. Consider the complexity of the eye. Does anyone really believe that this vastly complex organ evolved from a swamp?

Consider the female penguin. How do the females sometimes swim as much as 4,000 miles, return to the same hole in the ice and find their male partners with thousands of animals who look almost exactly alike. Contemplate the life-style of a beaver! Did the first beaver build a dam at night and under water, something it had never seen, without any help from God?

Think about how animals reproduce. Let's say two blobs of very complex cells come out of the primordial soup onto land. Let's say they decide to reproduce. (How did that happen?) Does one decide to be a male and one decide to be a female? Of course not! God created them male and female.

This world could only have been created by an infinite God, not by an accident. Evolution does change some characteristics; yet, evolution did not create the eye (nor to mention the remainder of the body) nor the penguin nor the beaver. The complexity of a single sell or DNA exceeds all mankind's knowledge and computer capability. Recognition of this fact should humble us!

Education is good and necessary. We must continue to learn and utilize our God-given abilities. Yet, when education - when knowledge - becomes our God, it is just as much sin, just as much a misplacement of our priorities, just as much a separation from Christ as any of the other more accepted sins of the flesh.

Intelligence and academic achievement are not in any way identical to wisdom and common sense. It is far better that our years help us develop more wisdom and common sense than putting more certificates of achievement on the wall. Wisdom is the skilled, honest use of knowledge.

In the long run, wisdom and common sense may give people more intelligence, less abiding fear, and fewer ulcers - folks who can enjoy a quiet hour in the sun, who can look at the earth and find it good, and who can think of the future and find it promising.

❦❦

The answers are in the Bible, not textbooks and universities.

❦❦

Ref. 1: Goodman, Peter S., "Taking Hard New Look at a Greenspan Legacy," NEW YORK TIMES, October 9, 2008, Pages 1.

13 END OF PROMISING CAREERS - ALCOHOL & DRUGS

"Anyone can see the kind of behavior that belongs to the lower nature are intrigues, drinking bouts, orgies and the like. I warn you that those who behave in such ways will never inherit the Kingdom of God."

Portions of Galatians 5:19-21

CHAPTER THIRTEEN

END OF PROMISING CAREERS – ALCOHOL/DRUGS

"Anyone can see the kind of behavior
that belongs to the lower nature are
intrigues, drinking bouts, orgies, and the
like. I warn you that those who behave in
such ways will never inherit the
Kingdom of God."

Portions of Galatians 5:19-21

The Board met at 10:00 am. The first order of business was to request the resignation of Virgil Hill, President of Valley Industries, and a Clothing Division of a major corporation. It took only a few minutes and Hill left the meeting, went home, had one drink, and then another and another. The next day the memories of his job, the distraught wife and embarrassed children brought him back to reality.

It all started five years ago. Virgil had been highly successful as the Manager of one of the firm's weaving mills. A friendly, outgoing fellow, he was liked by employees and management alike. His family was happy. They and their religion permitted drinking and drinks were served in the home to friends, to their teenagers and guests.

Then came the big opportunity. The Presidency of the Clothing Division became available. The Division had been purchased some years earlier from a family group. This was the company's chance to put in one of their own Managers. Virgil was the logical choice.

With little experience outside of manufacturing, he lacked the necessary skills to deal with marketing, distribution, styling, color and design of clothing. Yet, who was going to turn down an additional $50,000 per year? The business was profitable and the sales looked good.

Virgil took the job. Almost instantly friction broke out within management. Executives were jealous because they did not get the President's job. Virgil quickly found out that dealing with executives was different from dealing with manufacturing employees.

Drinks in the evening jumped from one to two or more. Then, a slowdown in sales and the profitable operations became losses. The Board was not happy. Soon there were one or two drinks at the Club for lunch. Next, the bar in the office was stocked with whiskey which was available all day.

❀

Soon the Executive Suite became known as the Executive Tavern.

❀

Virgil's decisions became less and less effective. Employees who could not tolerate this immorality began leaving the firm. Sales dropped and losses increased, resulting in the Board's action.

Many say that they can control their drinking. Yet, how many cannot? Others say that young people should be taught to drink in the home so they will know how to handle drinking when they leave home. But wouldn't it be great if they didn't drink at all?

Alcohol is one of the greatest causes of crashes on the highways. A significant number of deaths and injuries from automobile crashes are caused by drinking and driving. Alcohol - the most insidious drug - is a leading cause of executive failure in business.

When the business battle gets rough, when the crises arise - every person has a weakness - a possible breaking point. None of us know where that breaking point is or where it could be for us.

We will turn to our Christian faith, or we will turn to earthly retreats - alcohol, drugs, cigarettes or other excesses. We have been instructed to keep our bodies holy and acceptable to God. When the boss drinks, the other members of the organization probably will drink, too.

On earth, as a Christian - we are substituting for Christ, a mighty tall challenge and an important calling. Virgil Hill would still be the President of his Division if he had turned his problems, his crises, over to God rather than to the whiskey bottle.

Drugs and powerful prescription pain killers may be more damaging than alcohol, particularly with younger people. Consider the situation of Ben Payne. A teenager in high school in a small southern town in Florida, Ben was a tall and likeable teenager with a bright future. He was an outstanding pitcher on the baseball team in Junior High School. Coaches and scouts were confident that he would be recruited for a college team and then go on to the major leagues.

But, then a wayward sheriff's deputy illegally sold Ben, age 13, some drugs for recreational use. Immediately, Ben was addicted. Soon, he was arrested for driving with beer in his car and drugs for sale in his pocket. The time was the early 1970's, when Ben was seventeen.

His parents tried to help and became enablers. Rehabilitation treatment was tried over and over. The mother and father differed on how to handle Ben. His Mother always took the softer approach while his father wanted tougher discipline. In addition to all the agony of the family as Ben went in and out of city and county jails and state prisons, his parents marriage ended in divorce.

Ben's maternal grandmother, a nurse, drove her car off the road one night into a creek and drowned. Most thought the accident was suicide.

When talking with others, Ben always said what he thought that person wanted to hear. Often, he simply lied.

Sometimes, he would come to a relative's home and demand cash at odd hours. All gave it to him out of fear. Once, his mother requested $450 in cash from a cousin for Ben to pay a drug bill or the dealers would kill Ben. Drugs are available everywhere, even in some jails and prisons.

Now, at the age fifty three, Ben is in a state prison trying to get released for another time for rehabilitation. From seventeen to fifty three, he has been in and out of jail. The financial cost to taxpayers has been high. But, the cost to the family and the destruction of a marriage is even higher. Both parents are deceased.

Another young teenager in the seventies took too many and too much drugs. Today, he remains in a group home. His IQ is greatly diminished. His doctor said that he would never improve. The drugs had "fried' his brain. If anyone would look at the scans of the brain of a person taking drugs and one drug free, the differences and dangers are obvious to anyone.

Drug rehabilitation has a low record of success. Some programs claim thirty percent chance of keeping a participant off drugs for five years or more. The average rate of permanent addiction recovery is nearer one in eight. Whether a teenager, business person or a doctor, drugs destroy productive lives. Often, these twin devils cause brain damage, shorter lives and a greater chance of serious medical problems and some divorces.

So other than artificially feeling good for a short time, what is the reason for drinking alcohol and taking drugs? Sometimes it is caused by people with too much money and younger folks with too much stuff who cannot be satisfied with a simpler life.

The only real recovery is a changed person who accepts Christ. Then drugs and alcohol are not required.

☙❧

Rehabilitation without a
spiritual component is usually a
waste of time and money.

☙❧

2

14 POLITICS - RUNNING FOR PUBLIC OFFICE

"Truth is the only safe ground to stand on."

Elizabeth Cady Stanton (1815-1902)

CHAPTER FOURTEEN

POLITICS - RUNNING FOR PUBLIC OFFICE

"Truth is the only safe ground to stand on." Elizabeth Cady Stanton (1815-1902)

As Jim Jones and Stan Simons were having dinner in Montreal one night, Jim commented, "That's a very attractive Canadian flag pin you have on your coat lapel."

"Yes" Stan replied. "I wear it to make sure that no one mistakes me for an American." A loyal American and one very concerned about the values and changes taking place in his country, the comment was just like an arrow straight into Jim's heart. It could not be forgotten!

Upon return home from Canada, Jim received an unexpected call from one of the political parties. "We've got four good candidates to run for the County Commission. We'd like you to run for Chairman. A lot of people say they will support you."

Jim decided to think and pray about the matter; only five days were left to qualify. On the last morning of the qualification period, he paid his

$750 qualification fee and became one of the first candidates of the Republican Party to run in his county since the Civil War.

The Democratic Party had controlled the county since the Civil War. Jim was probably the first from his party to run for Chairman since that time. Most of his business was outside the county; so, he was free of some of the threats others would receive.

The party was running five businessmen - all had many years of business experience. Their qualifications were far superior to those of the other party's candidates.

Although never seriously involved in politics before, he naively set out to campaign. His business would not permit him much time, so he had to allocate the little he had to in order use it effectively. He assumed that "support" meant that those people who had recommended him would contribute to his campaign expenses.

He quickly found out that "support" did not necessarily mean help in any way - particularly, financial contributions. He enjoyed the opportunity to meet people, to speak to the various groups and participate in county activities. Many people came forward to help. The campaign was on a cash only basis. If there were no contributions, there was no promotion or any other activity that required money.

֎

*But, the rotten side of politics
quickly came to the surface.*

֎

A gasoline station owner told him one day,
"I thought you were a good fellow until you got
mixed up in politics." Many called to say they
would support him if he would promise to fix
some road or guarantee to fulfill some commit-
ment.

Accepting none of these bribes, he pushed
ahead with his campaign on a limited basis.

The owner of a local engineering firm called
to offer financial support and public endorse-
ment. Three days later, he called back to say,
almost in tears, "I cannot support you now." It
seemed that he had gotten word indirectly that
his last contract was from the state and it would
be a good idea for him to remember the source
of that contract when he decided whom he
would support for the county commission. If he
supported the wrong person, the next contract
might not go to him.

One of the candidates operated a trucking
firm serving the area's major industry. Industry people told him not to run. The industry
would put him out of business for running on

the wrong party ticket. He did not believe them, so he ran anyway.

In his campaign activities, Jim began to make sampling checks of those he talked with. It became apparent that one in three persons to whom he talked was not from his county. Another one in three people would not vote. Some did not even know that they could vote for a Republican.

More sampling checks indicated that only one in twenty persons whom he would meet at a shopping center or rally would know the name of either candidate or an issue in the election. This, he concluded, was a sad indictment of democracy. People were being elected to public office on the basis of publicity, name, and every other way - except qualifications.

It seemed to him that only three kinds of people would run for public office:

1. those that was financially independent and genuinely interested in better government
2. those who had something to gain financially by being in public office
3. those who are too naive or too inexperienced to know better

Jim fell in this third category. He was one who was foolish enough to think that the public really wanted better government.

The news media and others continued to press Jim to get to know the people. He did the best that he could with limited time and money. At the county fair, he would hand out cards. People would toss them on the ground. His two children would pick them up so they could be reused.

However, he always wondered why it was so necessary for him to get to know the people. Had it never occurred to the voters that they were the ones casting the ballots and that they were the ones electing officials to public office? It was partially their responsibility to get to know the candidates?

With scandals, disclosures, and indictments of many in political office and those associated with politicians - the distrust and lack of confidence in government had reached a low level.

Hardly any candidate has an opportunity to be elected without accepting large contributions from those who have the biggest bankrolls - industrial associations, business interests, unions, and other special interest groups. Upon election, he may find it difficult or impossible to say "No" to these big contributors.

The backgrounds of over two-thirds of the elected officials in state and federal government are believed to relate to legal services, and lawyers. The balance is certainly heavily weighed in those directions.

Business and businessmen must accept the responsibility for these inequities and these failures. Why? In pursuit of riches with the profit motive their number one priority and in climbing the business ladder - business and industrial leaders have isolated themselves, as individuals and as a group. They have not contributed their time and their talents to improving their community, their state and their nation.

It may be a matter of priority. In Jim's case, he had set his priorities to be:

1. Christ Jesus
2. family
3. country
4. business

Jim was a veteran of World War II and the Korean War. His country was high on the priority list.

☙❧

*Businessmen and Christian
businessmen in particular have
a responsibility to be involved in
politics, and to take a stand on the
important issues.*

☙❧

Politics, like business, is a great opportunity to help and serve others, and to witness to their Christian faith and their political activities.

Jim lost the election. His opponent received over 10,000 votes while he received over 3,000 votes. Not one of the five businessmen was elected. Name recognition and popularity won over qualifications and experience.

The election was in November. By March the next year, the candidate who operated the trucking business serving local businesses was out of business. The industry executives who threatened him when he decided to run were not joking.

15 Its SUNDAY - LET'S GO TO CHURCH

"Compromise plus committee equals collapse."

Unknown

CHAPTER FIFTEEN

IT'S SUNDAY— LET'S GO TO CHURCH

"Compromise plus committee equals
collapse." Unknown

"I don't know what the old Presbyterians believed and I do not care what the new ones say."

This is a statement of one of the laymen leaders in a local church. President of a major business, always in the forefront of civic activities, and Chairman of the Finance Committee, and Chairman of the Building Committee to construct a new church - such a statement points up the logic of many attending church for the wrong reason. It's the thing to do! It's good for business.

With no intent to judge,

☙❧

*it does seem that some men and
women take up religion for the
same reason they might take out
an insurance policy.*

☙❧

"It's nice to have something to fall back on, in time of sorrow."

Others may take up religion for the same reason they would detour a black cat on Friday the 13th. "There is nothing to this silly business, but a person might as well be on the safe side, just in case."

Others embrace the church for the same reason that they might embrace a rich uncle, "Who knows, this may pay off at some later date." Far greater numbers may drift into habitual church attendance for the same reason they might join a social club - because it is expected of them. It may not be a religious practice at all; it may just be a social habit. It is where some of their friends are on Sunday.

How many of us sit in church on Sunday morning and use the time to plan our business schedules for the following week? How many gaze out the window not knowing what the minister is saying? Or, on how many occasions are the utterances from the pulpit not worth listening to on Sunday morning? The devil can work just as well from the "comfortable pew" or from the pulpit just as easily as he can work in the executive suite.

Some church members stay in a church because they like the music. Some leave a church because they do not like the music. Many know only the position of there local congregation on issues. Many do not know where their denomi-nations leaders stand on issues like gay mar-riage or abortion or what takes place at national meetings.

Christ exists - or Christ does not exist. There, is no in-between, and there is no middle of the road. We either know what we believe or we do not. If one does not know what the early Chris-tians stood for nor care what the present ones say, we might as well join a social club, instead of a real church.

The Bible is either true or false. It is not a menu from which we can select the parts we like and discard those we do not care to believe.

A Christian businessman needs help from the church. He needs to hear from it the words of strength and encouragement to help him through the following week. The Christian business people are in the world all week long. Christians should be in the world but not of the world.

Managers do need to hear about Hell for Christ spoke more of Hell than Heaven.

☺☺

They do not need the prosperity gospel or liberal theology only.

☺☺

They need to hear the balanced Word of God.

The church is not a business - it is not to be run as an administrative entity. It should be 100 percent devoted to touching hearts and lives for Christ.

As the church builds assets, it often loses its target - its one mission. The one mission is to concentrate on bringing others to Christ so that they may have eternal life and minister to the needs of His children on earth. The one mission is not to build buildings, develop structures, nor do fruitless busy work in the form of organizational activities of administration.

Too often, a business person in church activities finds himself frustrated with the frequent and long meetings of committees. He or she is forever involved in compromise. It is an old saying; "Compromise plus a committee equals collapse." And this may be the reason that some church rolls continue to grow, while attendance declines and many drift away, spiritually or physically.

In an effort to be all things to all people, the organized church may be nothing to anyone. In an effort to be in the world, the church may be out of the world. It's an old saying, "the best way to clean up a pig is to get the pig out of the pen not get into the pen with the pig."

Christianity is to lift us out of sin, but not out of the world after we are born again with a new life in Christ.   "Eternal life is not something that awaits us in heaven. It begins here on earth when we commit ourselves to God and have Christ life placed within us" (Ref. 1)."

Ref: 1: Monod, Adolphe, AN UNDIVIDED LOVE, Translated by Constance K. Walker, AN UNDIVIDED LOVE, Solid Ground Christian Books, Vestavia, AL 35266, 2009, Page 73

16 THE SITUATION JUSTIFIES THE ACTIONS

"We are no longer to be tossed by the waves and about by every fresh gust of teaching."

Ephesians 4:14

CHAPTER SIXTEEN

THE SITUATION JUSTIFIES THE ACTIONS

"We are no longer to be tossed by the waves and whirled about by every fresh gust of teaching."

Ephesians 4:14

Tim Paine sells chemicals for Bedford Chemicals calling on garages, small businesses, and other small industries. A customer, Delong Maintenance and Repair, complains when quoted a $14.95 per gallon for a floor cleaner. He can buy it for $9.95 from a competitor.

Tim calls his boss, Bill Baines, and explains the situation. The boss says, "Sell it to him for $9.95." Tim asks, "How can we do that with our cost of over $10.00?" Bill says, "When we manufacture his order, we will just add more water to the mixing tank!" Is this ethical or situation ethics?

In all manufacturing processes, some products fail to pass in-plant quality tests or federal regulations. In the case of quality, the faulty items can be down-graded and sold at a loss or passed on to an unsuspecting customer, hopefully without detection.

Let's look at an example of a manufacturer of industrial chemicals. Federal laws protect the public against sub-standard products. To provide safe products will require discontinuing some existing items and increasing the cost of others.

As a manager, should we aid and assist the preparation and passing of proper safeguards? Or, should we resist, act through trade organizations and Washington lobbyist to delay, waterdown or prevent the passage of meaningful and needed legislation?

The situation is complex. Some interstate laws are in place because of corrupt policies or ignorance.

Assume a manager has fifty thousand dollars worth of goods in inventory which does not meet the new regulations and by federal law cannot be legally sold to the public in interstate commerce. Would he be justified in selling the products in intra-state sales or in delivering these intra-state, knowing they would be shipped interstate? Or, could the manager justify shipping the products to another country which did not have laws protecting the public?

The manager knows that other firms are not complying with specified testing requirements and are maintaining sales and earnings with faulty products. He knows, too, that many of his competitors will not manufacture their products to meet specifications, giving them a cost advantage. It is certain, too, that inspections are inadequate and checking and safeguards have not been made to uncover the offending firms.

National outbreak of salmonella which sicken 600 people is suspect in deaths of nine people results in the largest recall in US history (Ref. 1). Did the company knowingly ship contaminated products from two plants to avoid having to discard and take the loss on these suspect products? Was quality control inadequate? Where were the state and other public health inspectors? Were employees properly trained to make and test these products? How many of the employees were aliens – legal and illegal – who may not understand instructions in English?

An ethical manager is in between competition with their lower cost products and the legal requirements (and his ethical conscience). Do you wish to be sold an illegal product? Shall we recover the loss of our manufacturing mistakes from innocent people?

In the volatile, anything goes, world of business - sometimes it seems that there are no absolutes. More and more it has become the accepted thing not to speak the truth or to use half truths.

❀

A half truth is often worse and harder to detect than a lie.

❀

Business law is not honored if a way can be found legally around it, if the possibility of being caught is small. God alone gives us absolutes in right and wrong and the basis for truth in business.

God exists, or God does not exist. There is an eternity, or there is not. The statistical probability is either 1.00 or 0.00; there is no in-between. We must accept one or the other as the basis for doing business.

Much has been written and studies have been developed around the term "situation ethics." This is a belief that conditions surrounding a given situation determine the response for a person. A manager, faced with losses in operations which will lead to the termination of some of his people, might convince himself that in this situation, it would be better for him to deceitfully deliver an inferior product at a lower cost in order to keep his employees working. Though we should never deceive/delude the customer, using this approach, the situation determines the ethics - ethics becomes a variable.

Situation ethics is a dangerous game. With situation ethics logic, we can justify almost any action, almost any deal, and almost any decision. With situation ethics, managers find themselves in the whirlpool of indecision and quicksand is the foundation for their business.

Jesus Christ has compassionately set down the laws. He has set the example. Christian ethics - the same yesterday, today and tomorrow - are the foundation for a lasting business.

☙☙

There is no such thing as "situation ethics."

☙☙

Ref.1: Stengle, Jamie, "Tests confirm salmonella", THE TIMES, Gainesville, GA, February 26, 2009, Page 2C.

17 THE MISTRESS

"Marriage should be honored by all, and the marriage bed kept pure, for God will judge the adulterer and the sexually immoral."

Hebrews 13:4 NIV

CHAPTER SEVENTEEN

THE MISTRESS

"Marriage should be honored by all,
and the Marriage bed kept pure,
for God will judge the adulterer
and the sexually immoral."

Hebrews 13:4 NIV

The time was the mid-seventies. Jim Smith, age 40, was an outstanding sales manager for Oxford Chemicals located in Oklahoma. His business associates were always amazed how he could sell almost any product at the highest prices, even discontinued and off quality merchandise. And, his customers loved him.

After about five years, Jim decided that he could manufacture and sell his own chemicals and not be an employee of Oxford. With the financial help of some of his friends and customers, Jim bought property and set-up a manufacturing operation mixing and packaging chemicals largely sold to gas stations, schools and similar service businesses.

Sales grew quickly and the plant was expand-
ed several times to include the most modern
and automated equipment.   Customer service
was superior at Smith Chemicals.

Most of the customer service personnel were
ladies. Even though he was married and had
two children, one of the customer service ladies
always caught Jim's eye.

And, it was not long before Samantha was
promoted to Manager of Customer Service for
Smith Chemicals, now a multi-million dollar
business, a growing and profitable industrial
firm. Soon, Jim and Samantha were going out
to lunch together to "discuss business."

Even though the business was extremely profitable, it was almost impossible to get Jim to give
wage increases or benefit improvements to the
employees. As the years went by, Smith Chemicals employed more illegal immigrants.

Trade shows were part of the business. It was
not too long before Jim needed Samantha to
go to the shows and talk with customers. Almost
always, they traveled to the shows together to
Las Vegas, Chicago, Atlanta, Los Angeles, and
other cities. They stayed at the same hotels.

As time went by, customers, buyers and employees clearly saw that the two were together
more and more. Their relationship was the gossip of the industry. Samantha always got the

largest raises and the biggest bonuses. Her company car and all her expenses were paid by the business. When a job opened up in the firm, it was often filled by one of Samantha's family members or friends.

Jim's children knew what was going on. A son was an Executive Vice President in the firm. All were afraid to confront Jim. When his son asked how he could have this relationship given his marriage, Jim just said they were friends so it was not causing his wife any hardship.

Business lunches, dinners and trade shows soon developed into Jim spending more time with Samantha's than his wife. Many weekends and holidays, he told his family he would be away on business, but he was really with Samantha. He was living two lives.

Jim was a member of a main line church denomination. His attendance declined as the years passed. The situation continued as the decades passed. He always said he was a Christian.

At the age of 72, Jim had the opportunity to sell the business at an extremely high price, but Samantha opposed the sale. She knew that the sale would result in the loss of her job and the jobs of many of her relatives. The firm employed over 1,000 people in three plants.

Jim agreed to the deal and a date was set for closing. At the last minute, even though the buyer flew to Jim's office in Oklahoma City for the closing, Jim with Samantha's encouragement backed out and refused to sell. Jim wanted Samantha's love more than his business. Samantha with several relatives working at the firm wanted Jim's money more than his love.

The year was 2007. The month was November. As the financial crisis of 2008 developed, sales fell and the business became a loosing operation. Employees were terminated. Jim began developing memory problems. His wife of several decades had died earlier.

With new management taking the right actions, Smith Chemicals could have survived. But, Jim could not even think of turning management over to someone else, not even to his son who had been active in the firm for many years.

Even other managers, the Chief Financial Officer in particular, could see the handwriting on the wall - the company was going out of business. Jim and no one of his family could or would take actions to stop the slide into closure. After thirty five years in business, Smith Chemicals ended in closure. No buyer wanted it now.

It really did not matter to Jim or the family. Over the years, they had accumulated tens of millions of dollars and still owned the valuable real estate which could be leased for continuing income.

The losers were the loyal employees. Many of the workers on the factory floor had no place to go and ended up with nothing - not even a job. And there was no retirement plan.

❦❦

Most office romances start innocently.

❦❦

Two people become friendly; then they develop a relationship which leads to lunches, dinner, travel together on company business; and then the bedroom. Recently, a governor, mentioned as a potential candidate for President in 2012, explaining his South American affair at a news conference stated, "It all began innocently." It ended with his career and integrity in ruins.

Some result in divorce and remarriage. Here, the worst damage is done to the children and wife. Some go on for years with both individuals staying with their own spouses. Most think their husband or wife does not know of the relationship, but the truth comes out sooner or later.

With more women in business, the opportunity for office romances increases. Managers should set the example and take actions to avoid involvement or even the suspicion of an office affair.

There are procedures which can keep a reputation clean and avoid gossip in the workplace. First, never be alone in the room, or a meeting, or travel with a person of the opposite sex. This rule may require the office door to be open or be sure to invite another person in so there will be no cause for rumors to start. Sometimes, it may require traveling on different flights, in taking separate cabs, or staying in different hotels.

The Christian business person must make an effort to avoid a real relationship, suspicion or gossip.

◉◉

The Bible says that we are to abstain from the appearance of evil.

◉◉

18 SUCCESS - THE AMERICAN DREAM

"The true test of civilization is not the census, nor the size of it's cities nor the crops, but the kind of man the country turns out."

Emerson

CHAPTER EIGHTEEN

SUCCESS - THE AMERICAN DREAM

"The true test of civilization is not the census, nor the size of its cities, nor the crops, but the kind of man the country turns out."

Emerson

By all accounts, he was a good man. He had made it on his own. He was the town's United Fund Chairman, the church's cheerful giver, the bank's Board Chairman. He was a dedicated family man, and a regular at Rotary. When they wanted bible study in the classroom, he underwrote the cost. When they needed money for a new library, he was the first to give. Everyone knew him or knew of him.

His big white frame mansion with columns and giant boxwoods was on Main Street, two blocks from the courthouse. On weekends and vacations, he and his family would be flying to his seaside condominium. To all outward appearances, Bill Williams had it made. He had achieved success. For him, the American Dream was a reality.

Until March!

March was the month the commodity market lost its steam. Wheat, soybeans, cotton and other products reacted to a number of pressures, real and imagined. Soybeans, the protein rich darling of many speculators, soared to uncharted heights. But, Bill Williams was in soybeans on the short side. He had guessed wrong, investing money on the anticipation that the market would go down. Instead of going down, the price of soybeans had skyrocketed, costing him and his business thousands of dollars each day.

There was nothing to suggest that anything was illegal in his transactions. He had engaged in commodity trading in the past, earning money for the company. There was every Indication that his Board of Directors was aware of what he was doing. Slowly but surely, Bill Williams' world turned upside down. Within three to four short weeks, what had been the American Dream turned into his personal nightmare.

March 6th, just as dawn approached, searchers found his body beside the graves of his mother and father. His leased BMW was parked a few steps away. A 32 caliber pistol was close by.

"French Madoff investor found dead", was the headlines on the FINANCIAL TIMES, London (Ref. 1). The investor, age 65, had lost $1.4-billion in Madoff's Ponzi scheme. He apparently took his own life.

"Facing Losses, Billionaire Takes His Own Life", New York Times (Ref. 2). The German manager, once worth an estimated $9.8 billion, had speculated in the volatile Volkswagen stock and lost much of his empire. "The distress of his firm caused by the financial crisis and related uncertainties in recent weeks, along with the helplessness of no longer being able to handle the situation broke the passionate businessman and he ended his life." The businessman had signed some final documents dismantling his empire, walked a short distance to the railroad tracks, lay down and awaited the next train.

Bill and these other businessmen had everything. They had success in business, status and financial security. They had everything money could buy. Yes, they had everything and nothing. In the end, money, financial success and status are worthless.

❦❦

Everyone has a breaking point.

❦❦

We are all seeking, continually seeking success. But, what is success? What is at the peak of this mountain we keep climbing, ever higher, but never quite reaching the top? How will we know when we have succeeded in business, in management, and in life?

For years (thirty-eight to be exact), I thought that achievement in the world of business was success, an end in itself. Yet, the more I worked with executives at the top - the more I find that climbing the business ladder did not lead to peace, security, and satisfaction.

Five years ago, Jim Morrow was promoted to President of a major corporation. He had begun as a sales trainee two decades earlier. His one goal was to be the President of this company. His life was dedicated to that end. On the day his wife died of cancer, he had been in his OFFICE all morning.

Jim resigned his position and began his own small business with much less status, much less prestige, and much less income. At dinner one evening I asked him this question: "I know your one goal was to be President of that company, then, you resigned. Why?"

Jim's answer was,

◎◎

"I reached the top, looked around,
and found nothing there.

◎◎

I did not want to be a cog in the corporate machine."

On many days our business managers have breakfast with their families, meet with their staffs in the morning, solve an international problem over lunch; then, fly to a distant city for another business situation. The cell phone may ring 168 hours per week not to mention text messages, emails, and other communications. For most executives, a cell phone is not enough. They must have a Palm Pilot, BlackBerry or some other complex communications equipment always on hand. Compare this to our fathers who often walked to work, and were at all meals with their family. What does the future hold for managers in the over accelerated business environment?

Business management can be an opportunity to contribute to the world around us, to have a useful impact on human society and be an example for individual morality (which is given by Jesus Christ).

YES! A Christian can succeed in business.

Ref.1: Chung, Joanna, "French Madoff investor found dead," FINANIAL TIMES, London, December 24, 2008, Page 1.

Ref. 2: Doughtery, Carter, "Facing Losses Billionaire – German businessman, age 74, takes his own life," NEW YORK TIMES, January 7, 2009, Page B1.

19   SHE'S GONE – DEATH OF A SPOUSE

"All that we know about death can be found in the Bible. We who know Christ will rejoin our loved ones (in Heaven)."

Donald J. Barnhouse

CHAPTER NINETEEN

SHE'S GONE – DEATH OF A SPOUJSE

"All that we know about death can be found in the Bible. We who know Christ will rejoin our loved ones (in Heaven)."

Donald J. Barnhouse

It was 8:13 am on Saturday morning, September 23rd, 2006 that Anne's breathing stopped. She was gone!

On January 26th, 2003, Anne found a growth under her arm. The nurse in our retirement complex, Lanier Village Estates, sent her immediately to her Primary Care Doctor. Dr. Henson sent her straight to a surgeon. Biopsy results on the 28th confirmed the growth was cancer.

Surgery and lymph node removal confirmed Stage 4 breast cancer. On February 13th, 2003, Dr. Nash, our Oncologist reviewed Anne's test and performed an examination. He stated, "Anne, you have a few months to live. I recommend chemotherapy immediately for treatment which could gain some time." Anne replied with a confident smile, "If the Lord is ready, I am ready" and did not want to take treatment.

Dr. Nash told her that the cancer had spread over her body and into her bones. Without treatment, she would die a horrible death as the bones broke causing much pain. The only thing that could be done then was to knock her out with medication so she would not be aware of the pain.

After a week of thought and prayer, Anne decided to take the chemotherapy. The long path of treatments, tests and doctor's visits helped until August 2003 when the chemotherapy became too much and had to be stopped. Fortunately, the cancer had settled in her bones rather than a vital organ which would have resulted in an early death.

Radiation and oral chemotherapy helped her regain some strength. The years of 2004 and 2005 were much the same – treatments, doctor's visits and tests. Though weak, she was able to resume some normal activities including three trips to California on business with me.

The year 2006 started off with much hope that the cancer was controlled. Treatments were discontinued. But, the cancer returned. She was back in the hospital April 22nd, 2006 and September 19th, 2006. On the April 22nd, 2006 Anne fell in the hospital resulting in a severe concussion. Looking back, this accident was the beginning of the end. Never in all the hours of chemotherapy, the many blood draws, treatments or other activities did Anne ever complain.

There was at least one good thing that came out of my almost four years of being Anne's caregiver. We both got to know each other much better and the depth of our love increased with every moment we were together. I will always regret doing so many unnecessary and trivial things during our years before the cancer when I should have been with Anne.

A graveside service was held on September 25th, 2006 Anne had planned every detail. The bulletin for her memorial service, September 26th, 2006 was ready in the church computer. The date was inserted and the bulletin printed. Anne's preparation for her death with all the legal and other documents ready and updated in May of 2006 plus instructions to all involved was a significant help during this difficult time.

The memorial service was to the glory of God, not Anne. Rev. Richard Evans conducted the service and delivered a sermon Anne had heard and loved, "The Christian's Blessed Hope."

At 8:13 am on the 23rd, Anne's soul and spirit went instantly to be with the Lord. She was immediately fully conscious and aware of the presence of the Father, Son and Holy Spirit.

@@

She was never alone.

@@

We were married June 29, 1951. I was immediately recalled into the Army due to the Korean War. I had fifty five years of Heaven on Earth with Anne. But, that was not enough. Even though I knew that death was not far away for Anne, I was not ready!

The word of God tells us that Anne does not remember this earth's life and cares. The Bible shows that no one who has departed this life has any knowledge of what goes on here. Neither can the departed one hear us or come in contact with us. Even though there are no marriages in Heaven, we who know Christ shall rejoin our loved ones in Heaven (Ref. 1).

Activities following her death and people coming to visit plus cards and telephone calls kept me busy. Then, it all ended – I was alone.

Reading and studying the Bible plus other writings on death and the loss of a loved one was all I wanted to do at this time. I never knew what to say to people who had lost a loved one, particularly a wife or a husband. Now, I have found that others did not know what to say either. Everyone said to keep busy or take a trip.

Once, I thought that if one more person told me to take a trip, I would scream. The last thing I wanted to do was take a trip.

I found one thing that was helpful. Some would simply say, "I love you" and that was enough. I knew they understood.

Take good care of your spouse. You will not know until he or she are gone how much it will affect you. Every aspect of your life will be changed.

On some days, I might feel better and even move nearer being on the happy side; then, all of a sudden, for no reason at all, I would be overwhelmed with grief.

@@

Some call this event, "grief ambush"!

@@

Grieving is hard work. The sad days will always be with you because you loved, that is why it is sad. The gut wrenching sadness will diminish and become more reflective thinking instead of halting grief (Ref. 2).

I believe that women are stronger than men when it comes to grieving. Each experience of grief is unique. There is no textbook to follow.

Try as we may, we cannot put ourselves in the place of another suffering the pain of a loss. Often, the true and important things in life must be done alone.

A study by Jaap Spreeuw and Xu Wang of the Cass Business School, March 2008 (Ref. 3) concludes that in the year following a loved one's death, women were more than twice as likely to die than normal while men were six times as likely.

After fifty five years of "Heaven on Earth" with Anne, the world as I knew it came to an end; it was like an amputation. It was like starting all over again with no one to talk with about anything.

Try as we may, we are not prepared for the loss of someone we loved. Regardless of the depth of our Christian belief in life after death, we Christians go through this natural response to our loss. Though we knew for a long time that Anne would not survive, we maintained hope that medications would keep her here. I know she went through a lot to stay and love her family as long as possible.

The loss of a loved one we have enjoyed for a long time is hard enough. I cannot imagine the grief of a sudden, unexpected death, particularly of a younger wife or husband.

C. S. Lewis opens his book on the loss of his wife, A Grief Observed with this,

⊚⊚

"No one ever told me that grief was so much like fear.

⊚⊚

I am not afraid, but the sensation is like being afraid. At other times, there is a sort of invisible blanket between the world and me. I find it hard to take in what anyone says. It is so uninteresting. I dread the moments when the house is empty" (Ref. 4).

Some said time would heal the loss. Some said time would not help. I tried to keep up normal activities as if nothing had happened. It did not work. I kept everything in the apartment just as Anne had left it.

I looked at every slide, every picture, and every memory of Anne I could find. All of this helped, but the loss never went away. I told myself over and over that Anne was better off in Heaven glorifying our Lord with no pain or suffering any more, standing up straight, and being her beautiful self again. But, these kind of thoughts were good for about two minutes,

A helpful hymn was written by Thomas A. Dorsey (1899-1993) after the death of his wife. It is entitled Precious Lord, Take My Hand. Here are three of the verses:

Precious Lord, take my hand,
Lead me on, let me stand,
I'm tired, I'm weak, I'm worn;
Through the storm, through the night,
Lead me on to the light,
Take my hand precious Lord, lead me home.

When my way grows drear
Precious Lord linger near,
When my light is almost gone,
Hear my cry, hear my call,
Hold my hand lest I fall,
Take my hand precious Lord, lead me home.

When the darkness appears,
And the night draws near,
And the day is past and gone,
At the river, I stand
Guide my feet, hold my hand,
Take my hand precious Lord, lead me home.

Dwight L. Moody's death was recorded by James Montgomery Boice (Ref. 5). The morning of his death, his son was at his bedside and heard him exclaim, "Earth is receding, Heaven is opening; God is calling." "You are dreaming Father." Moody replied, "No, Will this is not a dream. I have been within the gates. I have seen the children's faces." For awhile, it seemed that Moody was reviving, but then he began to slip away again. He said, "If this is this death? This is not bad; there is no valley. This is bliss. This is glorious." By this time his daughter was present and began to pray for his recovery. Moody said, "No, no, Emma, don't pray for that. God is calling. This is my coronation day. I have been looking forward to it." Shortly after that, Moody was received into Heaven.

I live because of the certainty of my salvation due to Jesus Christ forgiveness of my sins, and I know that every day brings me one day closer to Heaven when I will glorify the Lord and be with Anne again. There are no marriages in Heaven (Mathew 22:30), time and night do not exist (Rev. 21:22-27), but I will be with Anne (Ref. 6) and all the others who have gone before and those who come after me for eternity!

The hole in my heart grows smaller with time.

☙

But, the hole will never be filled here on earth.

☙

Our minds are too small to know the greatness of God and His Heaven.   As Adolphe Monod said as he was dying of cancer, "Life is good.   Death is good because it frees us from the miseries of this life and above all because even if life for us was filled with all the joys that earth can give, death causes us to enter into a joy and glory that we cannot even to begin to imagine"   (Ref. 7).

Author's Note: This chapter is true.   Names, dates and places have not been changed.   It is my story.

Ref.1: Barnhouse, Donald Grey, "Death Is Swallower Up In Victory," Alliance of Confessing Christians, Philadelphia, PA, www.AllianceNet.org., Revised 2007.

Ref. 2: Rogers, Valley, E-mail, June 24, 2007.

Ref. 3: Jones, Sam, "Of couples and copulas," FINANCIAL TIMES, London, April 25, 2009, Page Life & Arts 1.

Ref. 4: Lewis, C. S., A Grief Observed, 1961, Harper Collins Edition, 2001, New York, NY, Page 3.

Ref. 5: Boice, James Montgomery, Philippians, Baker Books, Grand Rapid, MI, Fourth Printing, July 2004, Pages 223-224.

Ref. 6: Boice, James Montgomery, The Gospel of John, Volume 4, Baker Books, 1999, Page 1069.

Ref. 7: Monod, Adolphe, Living In The Hope Of Glory, Paris, 1856, Translated by Constance K, Walker, P&R Publishing, Philipsburg, NJ, 2002, Page 60-61.

20 HE'S GOT EVERYTHING – AND NOTHING!

"Men will wrangle for religion-, write for it;
fight for it; die for it; anything but live for it."

Colton

CHAPTER TWENTY

HE'S GOT EVERYTHING - AND NOTHING!

"Men will wrangle for religion;
write for it; fight it; die for it;
anything but live for it."

Colton

The whole manager must look outside the business world to keep abreast of changing times and conditions. In addition to business, many of us have looked to other things than our vocation for success - education, theology, or government – and as the answer to all our needs.

Sometimes, we tend to think that a college degree or some other certificate, diploma etc. on the wall will solve our longings. Some think that if we, if mankind, could just be educated, the world would be a better place.

Some think that science will replace religion. There is no real conflict between science, the Bible, and Jesus Christ. The fact that man has gone to the moon is trivial in the infinity of space. The more one learns, the more one realizes the minuteness of a man's knowledge, of man's achievements relative to the mightiness of the earth's systems, of life; the world could only be created by an all knowing God.

In our present time, there is much talk about new theology. Many of us have read books written by the proponents of the various new theologies – the New Age Movement, situation ethics, God is dead, and others. Some have turned to drugs and alcohol.

Some decide that parts of the Bible are true, that part of it are allegories, that parts of it are fables; then take from it those things they find convenient and leave the rest. Any time we make a change - and change is good - we need to replace whatever we tear down with something better. If we tear down a person's theology we need to offer him a better one.

This is the real flaw with the new theology. It tears down the validity of the Bible and does not replace it with something better. There is nothing better. It destroys the moral foundation of the Ten Commandments by means of a permissive society. It does not give us a basis for living.

Probably the greatest myth facing us today is the belief that governmental systems can solve the problems facing businesses, and facing mankind.

Some socialistic nations are ideal examples of governmental involvement in the lives of people and business. In some countries, much of industry is nationalized - factories, motels, and hotels. There are few strikes, for the terms of settlement are generally dictated to both union and management by the government. There is little or no material poverty for people at any level-blue collar, management, or unemployed.

Medical services are equally available to all under the socialized medicine schemes. For a small sum, a person can get any medical attention - from a broken finger to brain surgery. The cost is the same regardless of the length of hospital stay, medication required, or equipment needed.

One of these nations has provided so well for its citizens that one of my friends there has said, "There is no need for God. The government provides everything." Is this the direction in which the United States is going? Will it answer the searching needs of mankind?

When a human being has his material needs satisfied, his educational goals attained, and his medical services provided, the environment may be excellent. Yet, the real need is to satisfy the heart, the soul, and the mind. It is essential to eliminate anxiety and insecurity. It is necessary to find a basis, and a meaningful foundation for living.

After spending thirty-eight years of my life chasing success–in business, in school, in theology books, in government–an event occurred in my life which was of vital importance. I had been going to church, an Elder in the church, teaching Sunday School, and putting up the front required of a good church member.

The date was December 21st, 1966. The time was 10:05 am. Anne, Lynn, Chip and I were on our way to Bishopville, SC from our home in Gainesville, GA to spend the Christmas Holidays with Anne's parents. As we came over a hill about 10 miles from home, a teenage girl driving a pick-up truck drove off the payment onto some wet grass. When she applied the brakes, rather than just driving back onto the payment, the pickup truck skidded into our car with a head on crash.

With every member of the family hurt, my son's brain possibly damaged from a concussion; internal bleeding and a broken back causing my wife's life to be in the balance; my daughter injured with a severely broken leg and myself injured (with a badly mangled broken left arm and broken right hand) –

for the first time in my life, I was not in control.

Gas was leaking out of the car; yet, people would come up smoking and look into the car at the injured family. A State Patrolman arrived and got everyone away and stated, "We have got to get these people out of the car – it could explode." Everyone said the doors were jammed. He walked up to the right front door and literally tore it off the car.

Fourteen doctors, many I did not even know, provided medical care. People took care of everything, and the prayers of many changed our lives. Prisoners in the local jails came and gave blood for us. Chip's mouth was badly mangled and his teeth were significantly damaged. A skilled dental surgeon from Atlanta closed his office December 23 and came to Gainesville. He worked on Chip's teeth for seven hours and not a tooth was lost.

As time progressed, everyone recovered, but injuries remained forever. The driver at fault never paid a penny of the cost or damages. Our health insurance plan paid about $7,000 and cancelled the policy. Having started my own consulting business in 1963 and working alone, income ceased. Bills pilled up.

The President of a local bank called me in the hospital one day and said, "We have opened a checking account for you". Startled, I said what collateral do you need. He said, "None". Then I said, "What is the limit on the account?

He said, "It is unlimited". Write all the checks you wish for any amount". Then, I asked about paying back the loan since I worked alone as a consultant and would not go back to work anytime soon. He replied, "It does not matter when or if you pay it back". One client sent a check for $7,500 and a friend added $2,500. It would be almost five years later that all bills were repaid. Adjusted for inflation, this $10,000 in 1966 would be approximately $65,000 in 2009.

Out of work for nine months, the bills and loans pilled up. It took years to repay all the monetary cost of this accident.

The 1960's was the time when Nietzsche's "God is dead" theory was popular. God is alive and well in 2009. Where is Nietzsche (Ref. 1) and those who adopted his theories?

In my younger days in business, I thought that Managers and Presidents of businesses were essential to the success of firms. As time went on, I learned that there are no essential people in business. After a personnel change, management and the company often go on as usual, sometimes even better.

@@

The fact is that everyone is expendable.

@@

I used to go to religious retreats on weekends and wonder why so many speakers stood up and told of tragic events from which prayers were answered. I wanted to know if there were any Christians who had found Christ without tragedy. Now–I know. The harder one's head is, the harder he must be hit to get the message.

The message is that Christ is in control. Success does not originate in business, education, especially financial possessions or theology. These things seem insignificant when one has a severe problem.

It is necessary for us to earn a living, for our lives to be productive. Yet, when business becomes our God, we are aiming at the wrong goal; we are aiming at an incomplete life.

I found out from that automobile accident that Jesus Christ (who is God, the Son) is the only hope of the world, mankind, and societies. Although I have not reached the mark, though I sin every day, I know Christ is alive, that the goal is not life on this earth - the goal is to be with Christ in eternity. The chief purpose of man is to glorify God and enjoy him forever.

There are some things in life we must do alone. Try as we may, we cannot put ourselves in the place of another who is racked with pain, in the executive suite of a manager with a complex business decision, in the situation of losing a spouse after decades of happy marriage or in the heartache of a loved one.

❦

Life is a continuous series of events and decisions from which there is no turning back.

❦

Once, while flying to New York, I was sitting adjacent to a flight attendant. It happened that both of us were flying on across the ocean, she to Rome, and I to London. In route, she was telling me about her next trip. She had four days of vacation. She was going to fly all night, be in Rome one day, and then fly to Zurich, fly back to Rome, and then fly home. If this weren't enough, on her next four days off, she was flying to Hong Kong to do her Christmas shopping. With the airline travel to Hong Kong, she would have less than twenty-four hours on the ground to do her Christmas shopping. This did not make sense!

As we were landing at Kennedy in New York, she said, "I have not told you the truth. I am running away." It turned out that the young man she was to marry had died unexpectedly of a very rare heart ailment. She said,

@@

"I can't stand to be alone - alone
in my room."

@@

We do not have to be alone in our room, alone in the executive suite, alone on the factory floor, alone on the sales call, or alone in our management group.

There were years when I presumed to weigh the Christian faith, the teachings of theologians, and all religions - and define them as equally wanting. I can say this without embarrassment today, and without apology. I fail to see how any person with reasonably normal intelligence could have reviewed the same evidence and reached any very different verdict.

I was never satisfied with my role as a management consultant - struggling to find a safe pathway in management - to lead a few lost souls out of the business wilderness. The fact was that far too little was being done to keep them from getting lost in the first place.

At one time, I believed that perhaps I could read, study and accumulate enough knowledge - listen and learn until I could perfect an authoritative description of management. I dreamed of writing a handbook that would be simple, practical, easy to understand and easy to follow.

It would tell people how to manage - what thoughts, attitudes and philosophies to cultivate, and what pitfalls to avoid. I attended every seminar it was possible to attend. I read every book. I took notes on the wise words of my teachers and my colleagues who were leaders in the field.

Then, quite by accident, I discovered that such a work had already been completed. I know that the following is true.

If you were to sum the total of all the authoritative articles ever written by the most qualified experts in the field of management, if you were to combine them, and refine them, and leave out all the excess verbiage - if you were to take the whole of the meat and none of the parsley, and if you were to have these unadulterated bits of pure knowledge concisely expressed by the most capable leading writers, you would have an awkward and incomplete summation as a step by step guide to management which has already been set down in the Sermon on the Mount (Mt. 5-7). All management books suffer immeasurably in comparison to the Sermon on the Mount.

☙❧

Here, rests the blueprint for
successful management, for
contentment in human life

☙❧

(Ref. 2)!

We cannot continue indefinitely yearning for peace while anticipating war; groping for love while indulging in hatred; struggling for security while building insecurity, or using drugs and alcohol to relieve stress. We cannot live forever in fear of imminent nuclear annihilation or terrorist attack; lest that fear extract a higher toll than the potential bombs themselves. Hopefully, man will learn to live a simple and satisfying life in harmony with himself and his fellow man, because sooner or later he will have no other choice. No one will find it except in Christ and then only when our salvation is complete.

Man must learn to live a more satisfying life with less abiding fear, less nervous tension, and greater freedom from feelings of guilt and helplessness. He must find self reliance and self respect.

Jesus and the great philosophers, the great thinkers, the great religious leaders of the world, almost without exception, have warned of the perils of pursuing earthly treasures. They have earnestly recommended the simpler life. Many historians have concurred, for the rise and fall of empires can be traced in the pattern of collective wealth and individual helplessness.

Personally, I am not discouraged! Man's groping for a better kind of life grows more frantic as he becomes more desperate. Simple truths cannot remain forever hidden, and a false position sooner or later becomes apparent?

For the first time in many years, people–and particularly young people–are turning to Christ through Young Life, Athletes in Action and Campus Crusade for Christ. Christian Colleges plus other groups with other witnessing methods are teaching people how to pray and live. The lessons of the scriptures are breaking through. When a man can recognize his responsibility to contribute to the world, he has learned to love, rather than attempting to exploit others for his own advantage; when he has a bond of kinship with all people - then, he will have found the key to contentment and secret to a satisfying life. The years teach much the days will never know.

It is not enough for man to learn theology, quote proverbs, read the books of great religious leaders, or find religion. They must find Jesus! God must take these lessons and weave them into the fabric of a man's life. In a world torn by war, by insecurity, by changing values and by expanding management demands, is it possible to be Christian in business and succeed?

YES!

I believe that for nearly 2, 000 years, the Christian world has been holding in its hands the complete answer to our restless and fruit-less yearnings. Here, with Christ, rests the blue-prints for success in human life.

If God were to ask you, "Why should I let you into my Heaven?" What would you say? If you are not 100 percent certain pray, "Dear Lord Jesus. I know I am a sinner and do not deserve eternal life. But, You loved me, so much that You died and rose from the grave to purchase a place in Heaven for me. I now trust in you alone for eternal life and repent of my sins. Thank you for your gift of eternal life!"

Ref. 1: Nietzsche, Friedrich Wilhelm, Nietzsche & the Death of God, Bedford Books,

Ref. 2: Fisher, James T. and Hawley, Lowell S., A Few Buttons Missing, J. B. Lippincott Company, New York, 1951, Twelfth Printing, Page 273.

4298888

Made in the USA
Lexington, KY
12 January 2010